I0845183

I am grateful to God for everything! And I believe that the meaning of life is to make sense of other lives. C.A., you are the meaning of my life.
Lov U

Joel Gomes
2023

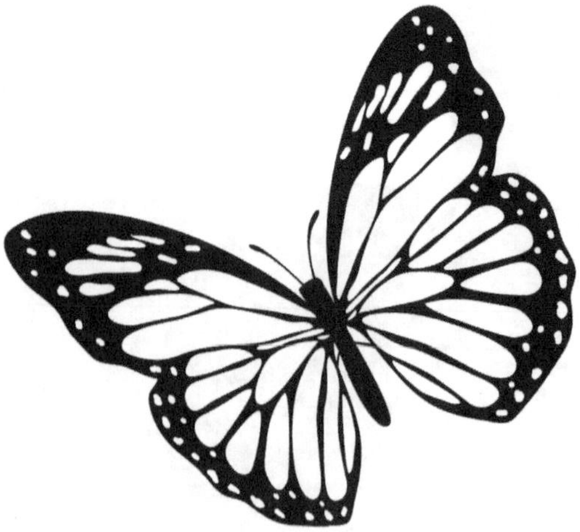
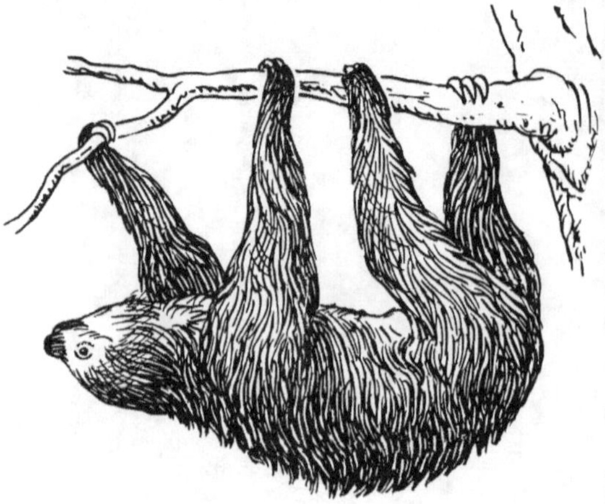

This Book Belongs to:

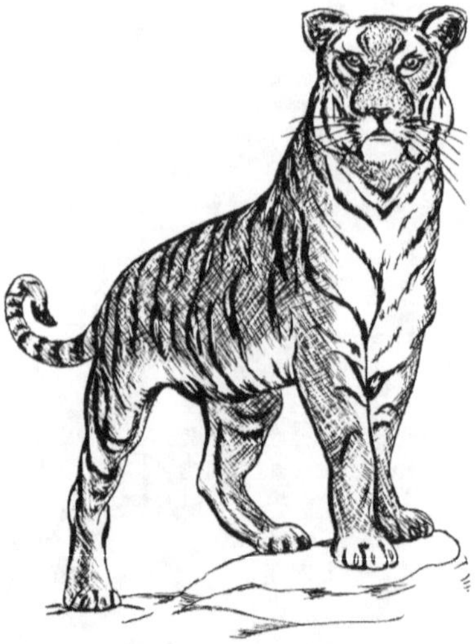

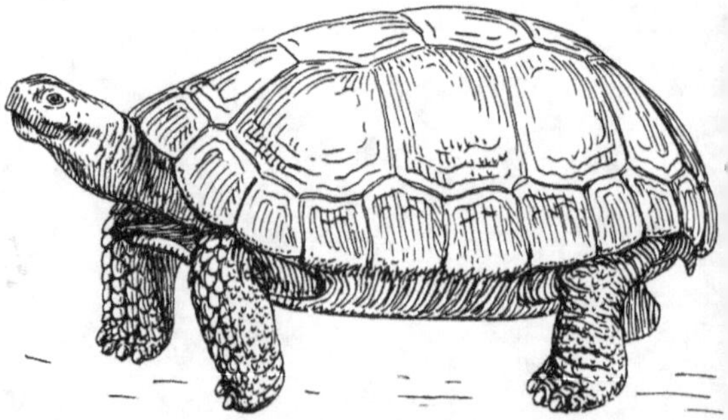

J.G.P.©
JoelGomes publications

Test Color Page

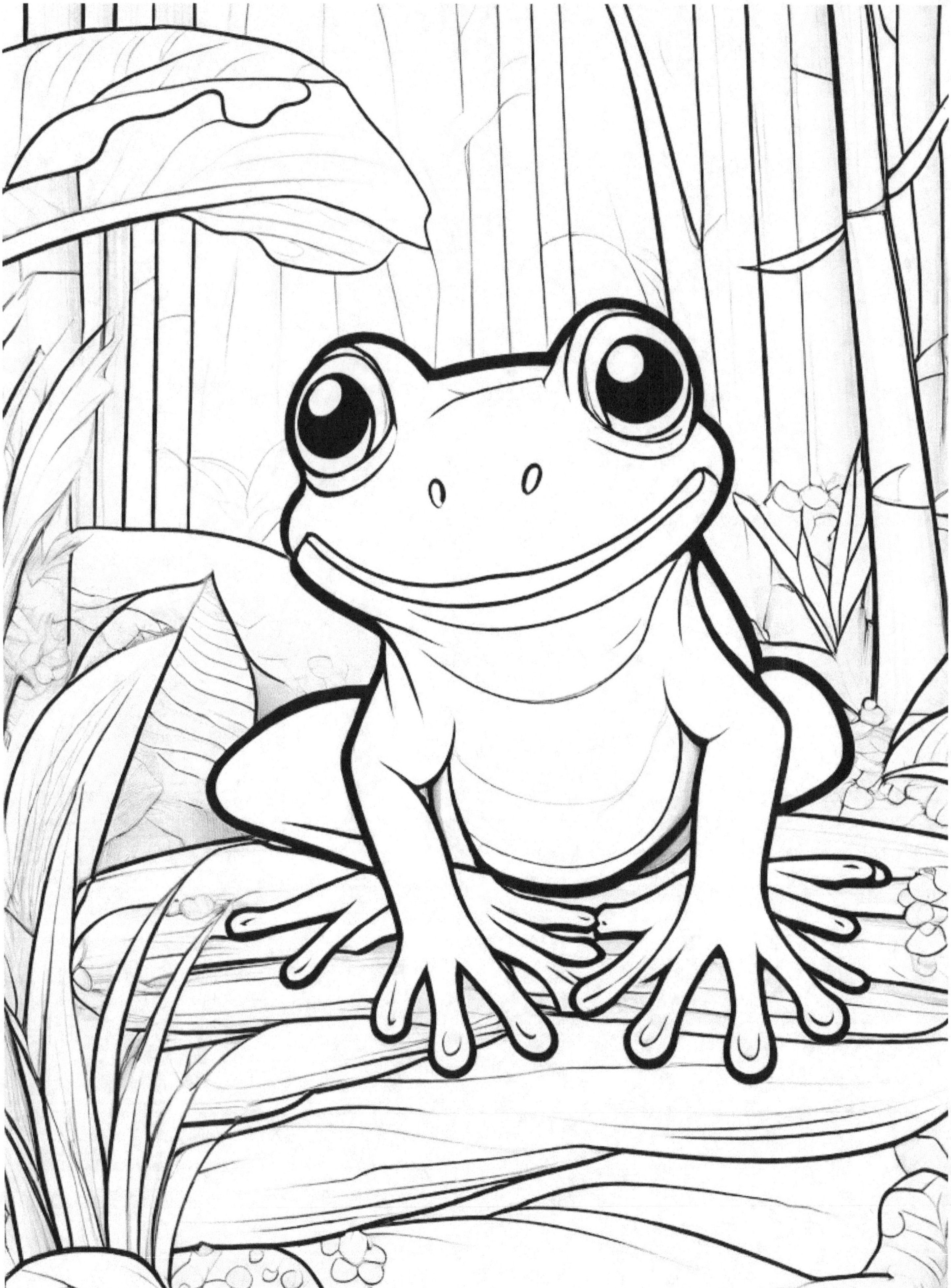

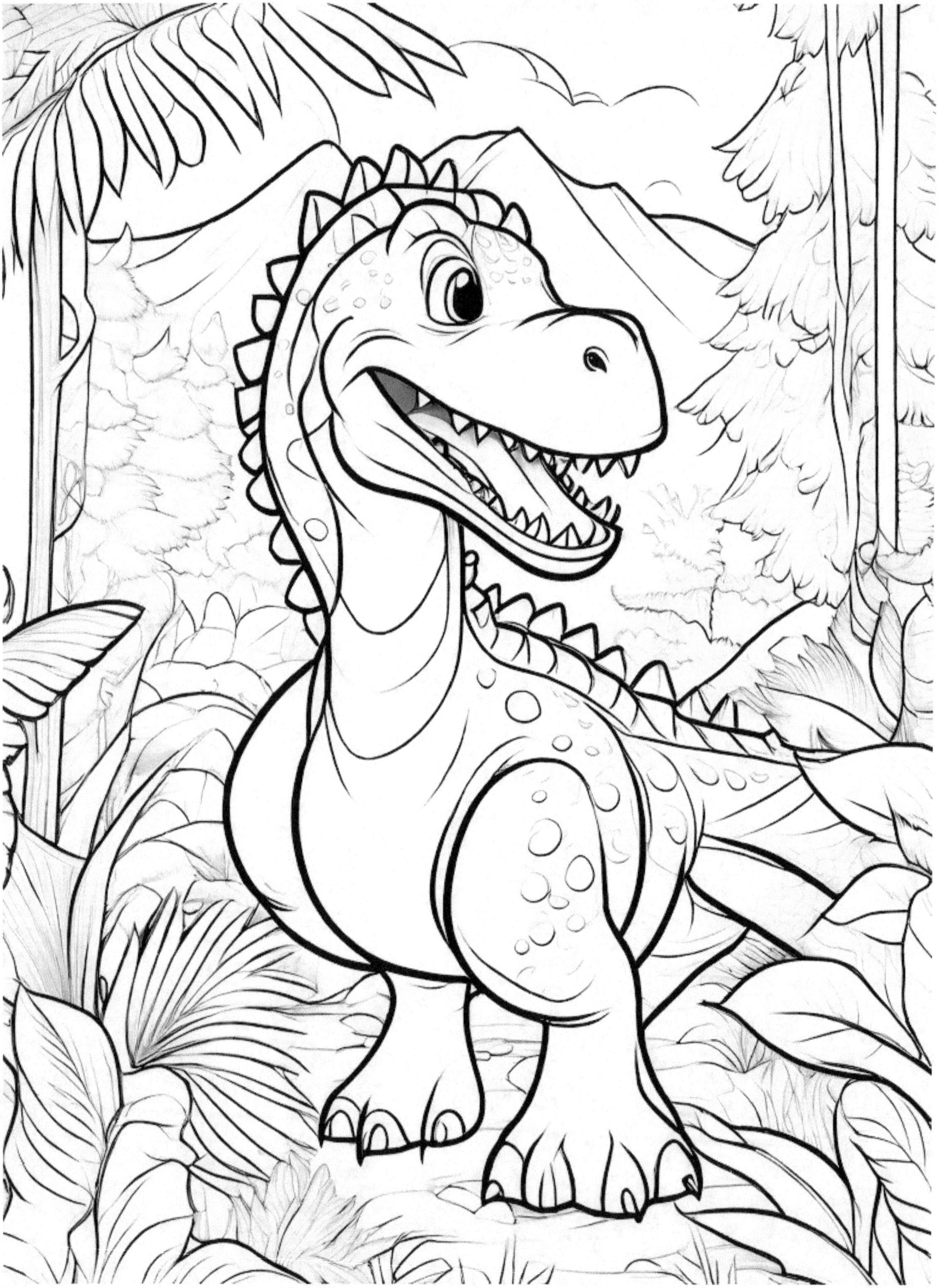

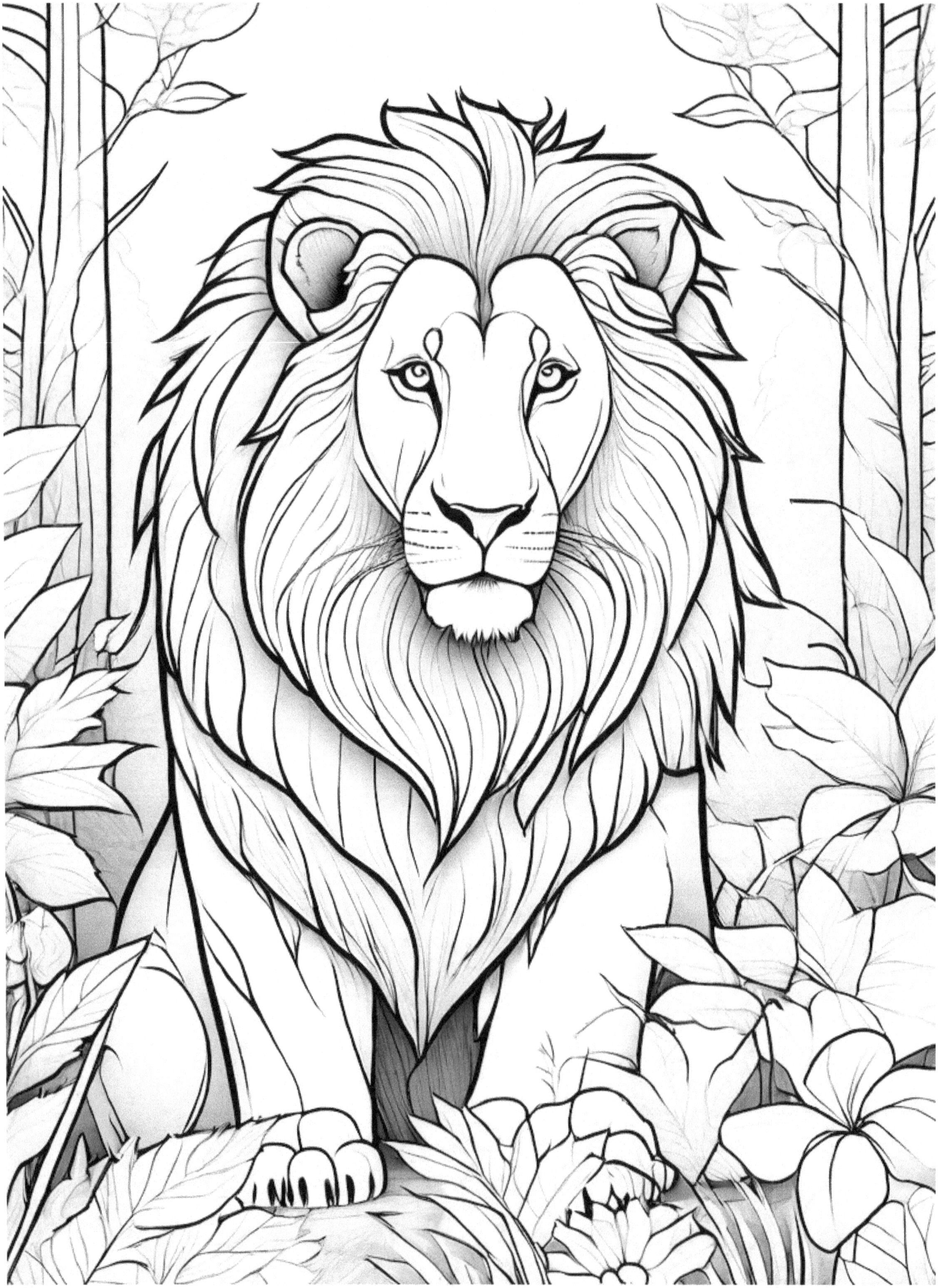

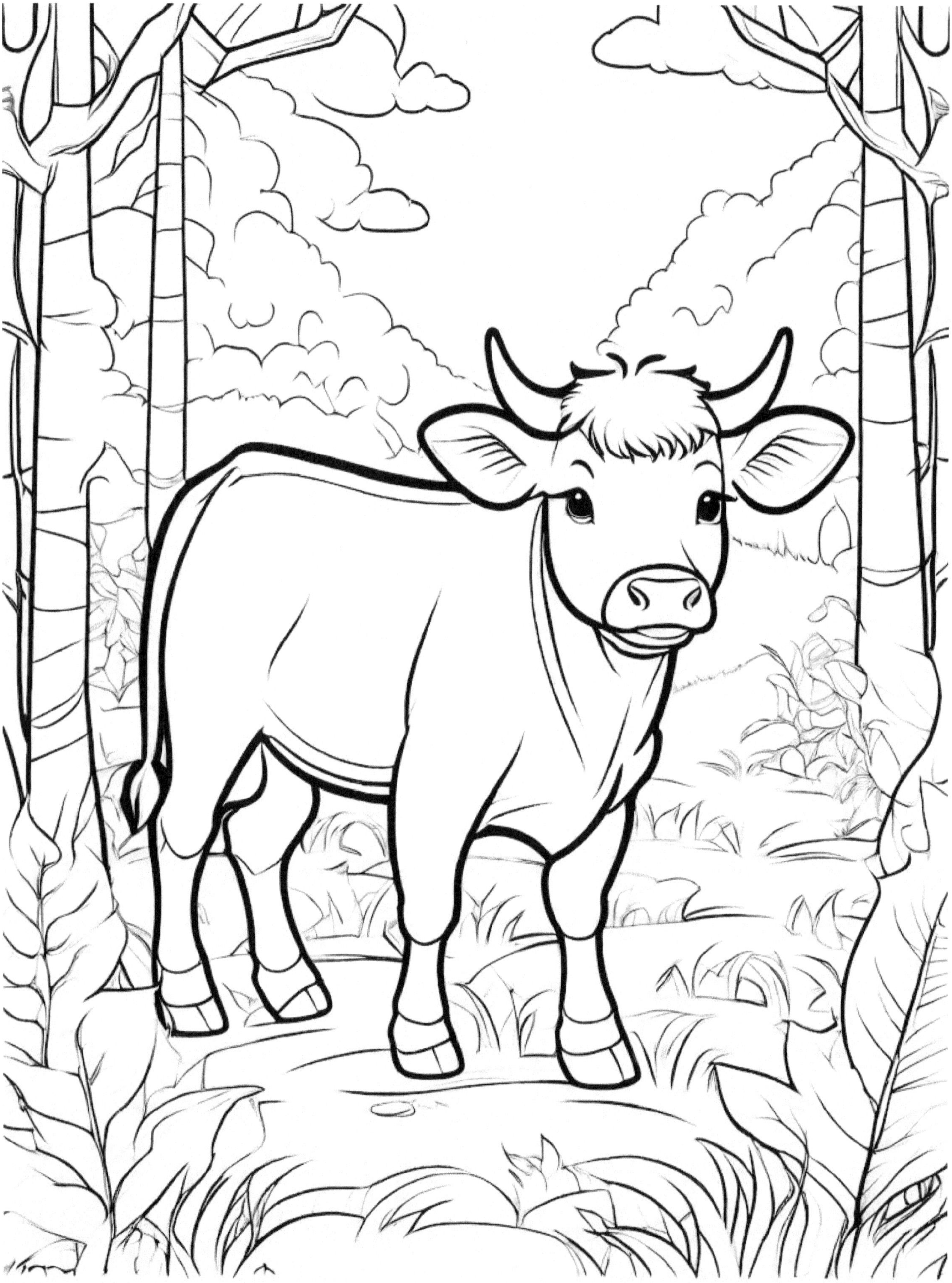

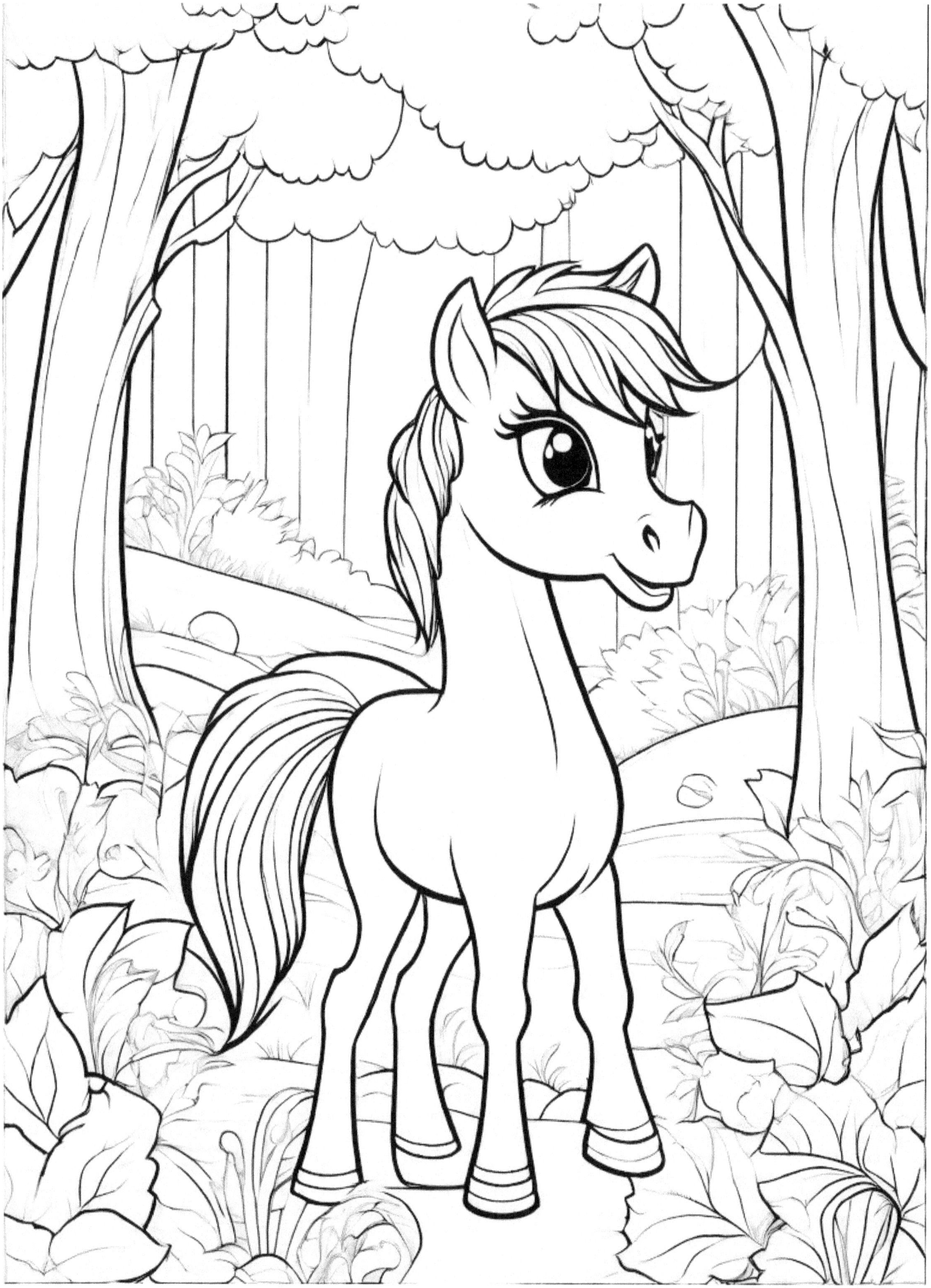

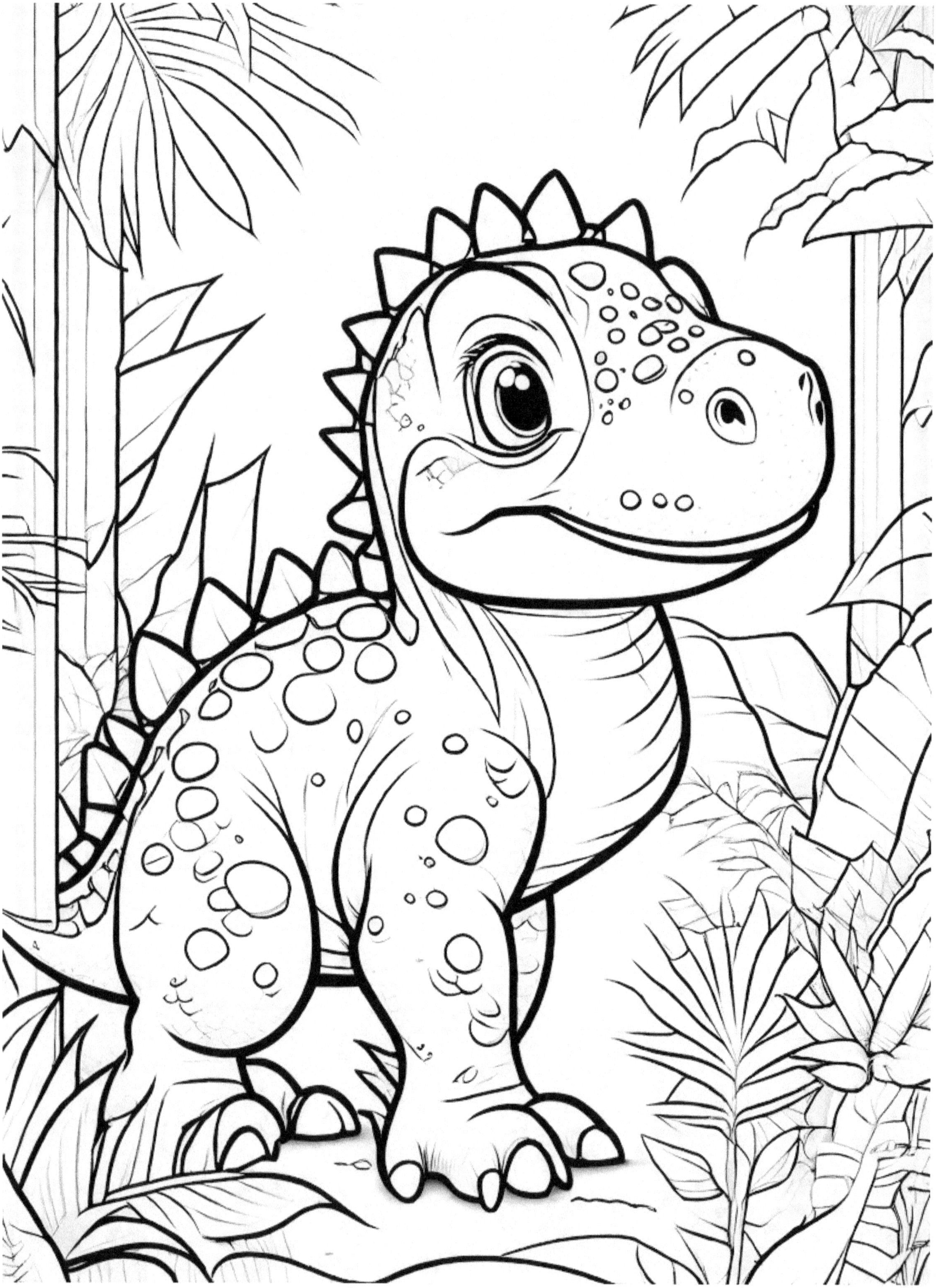

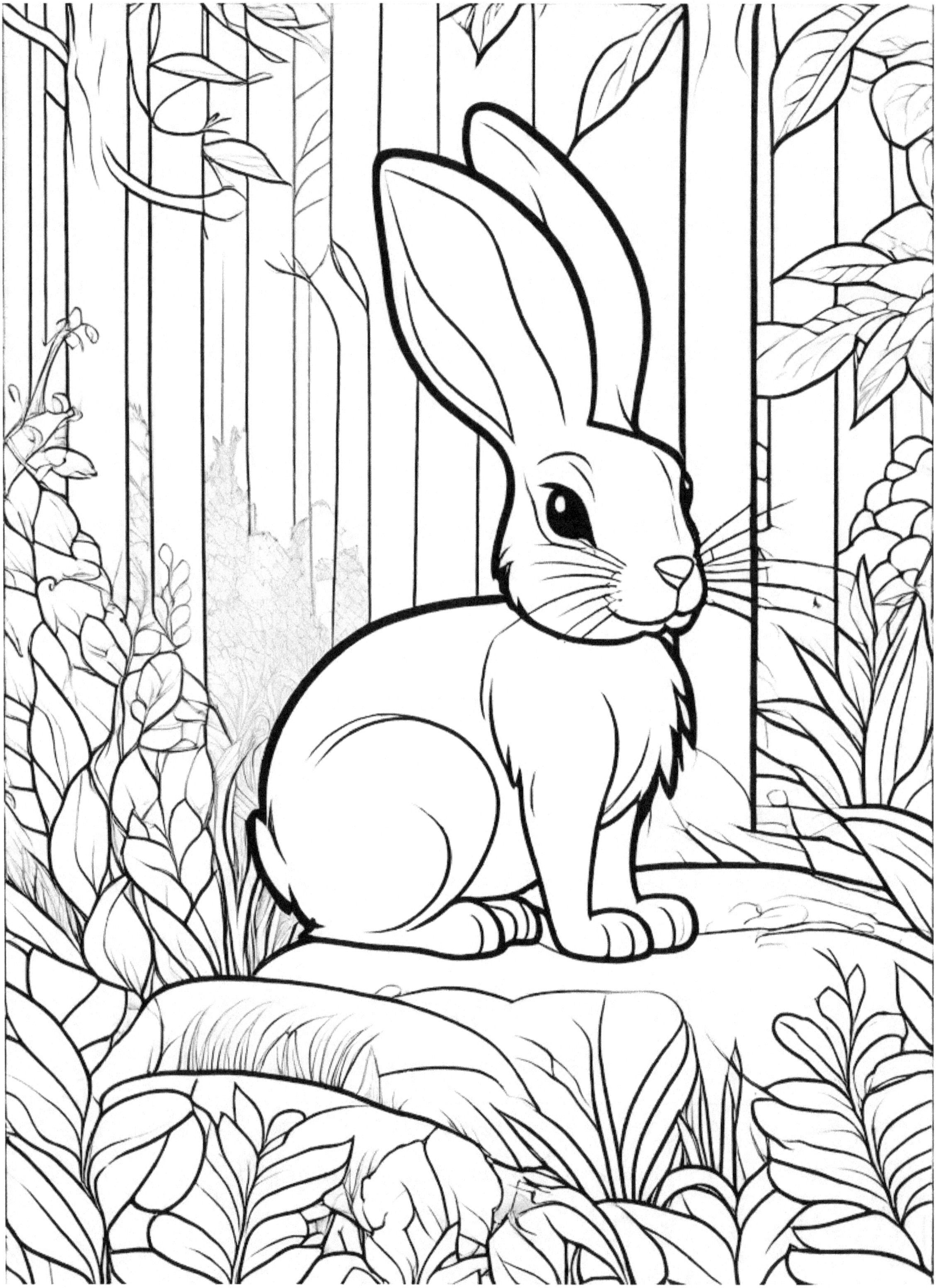

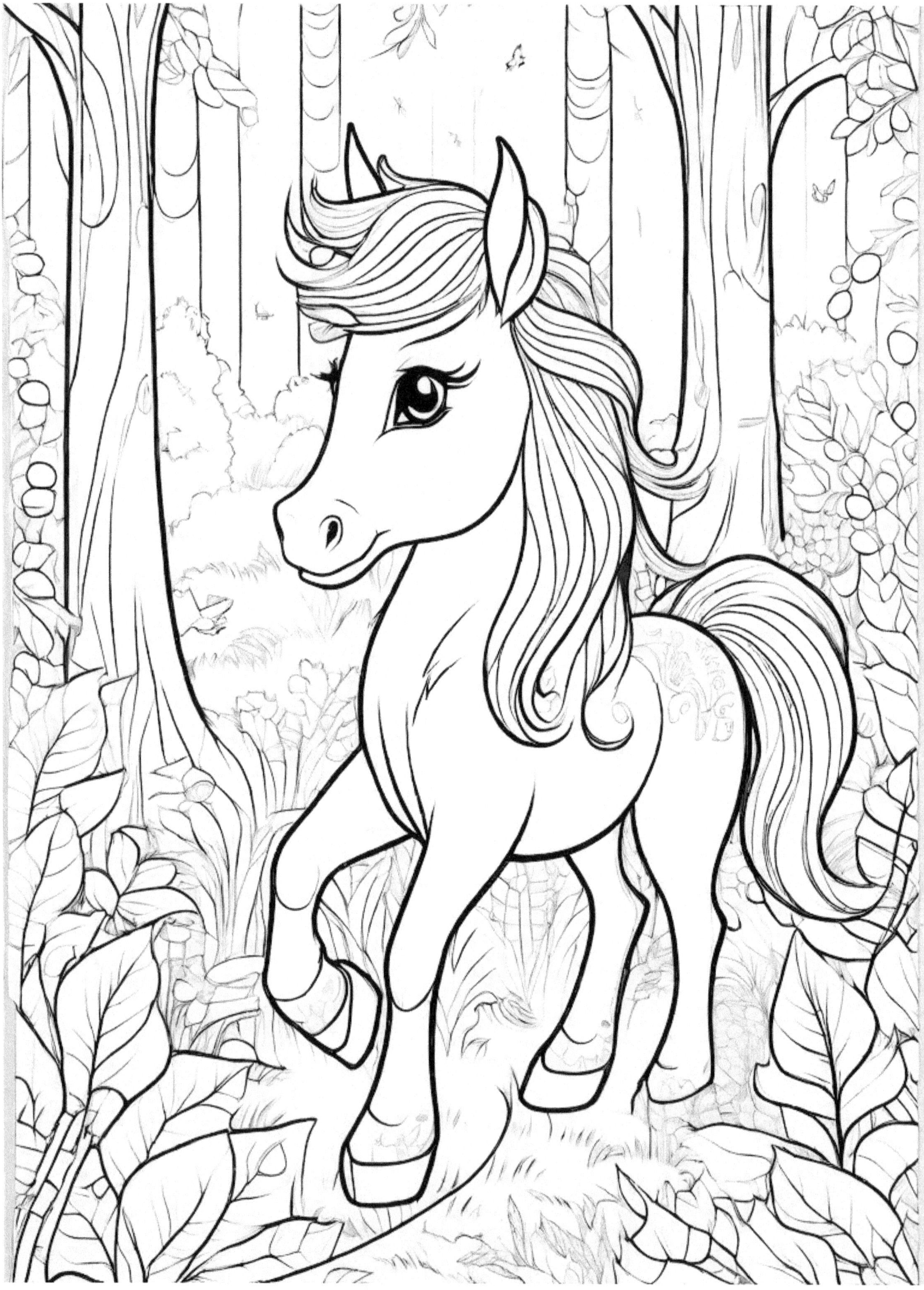

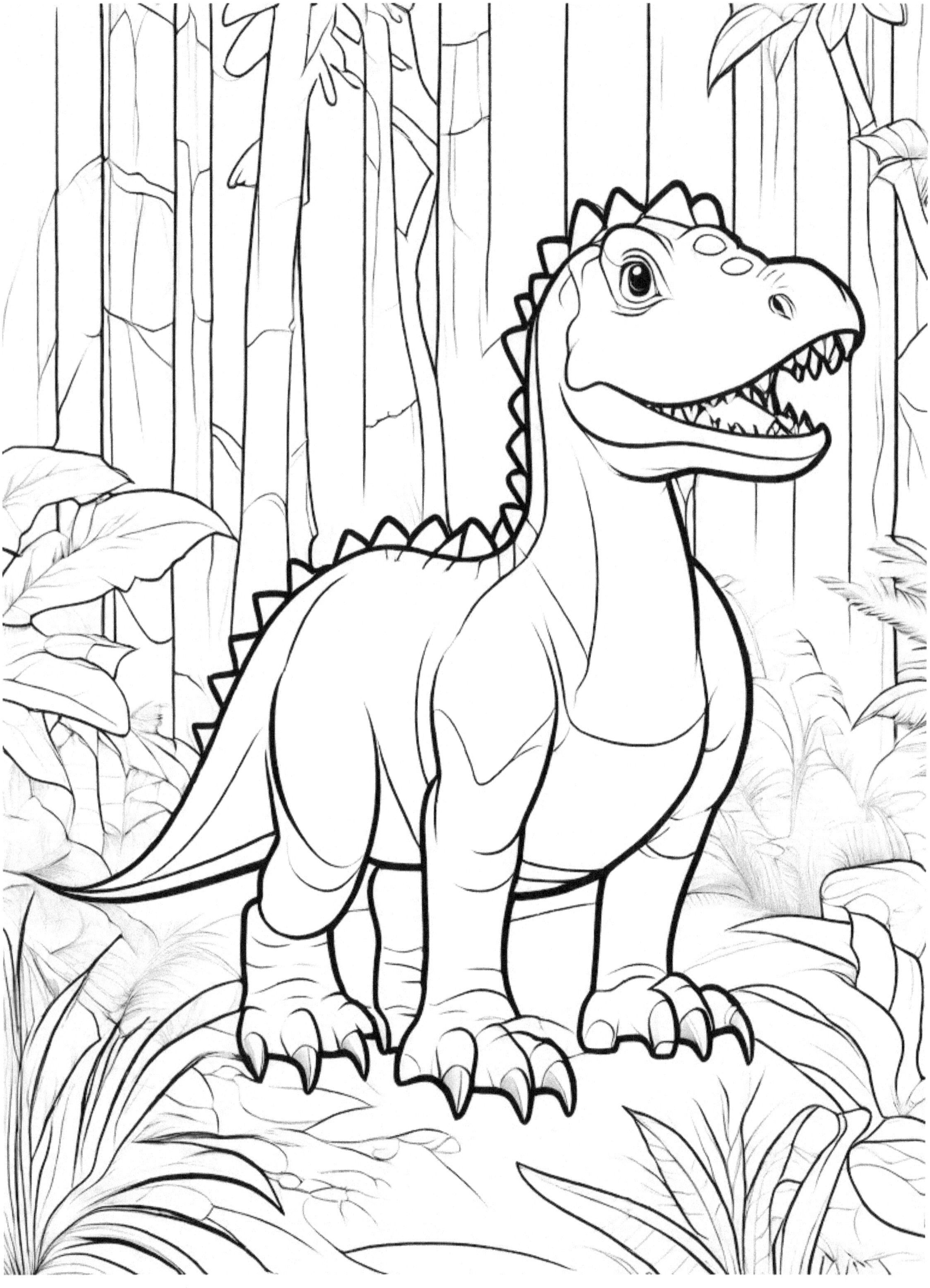

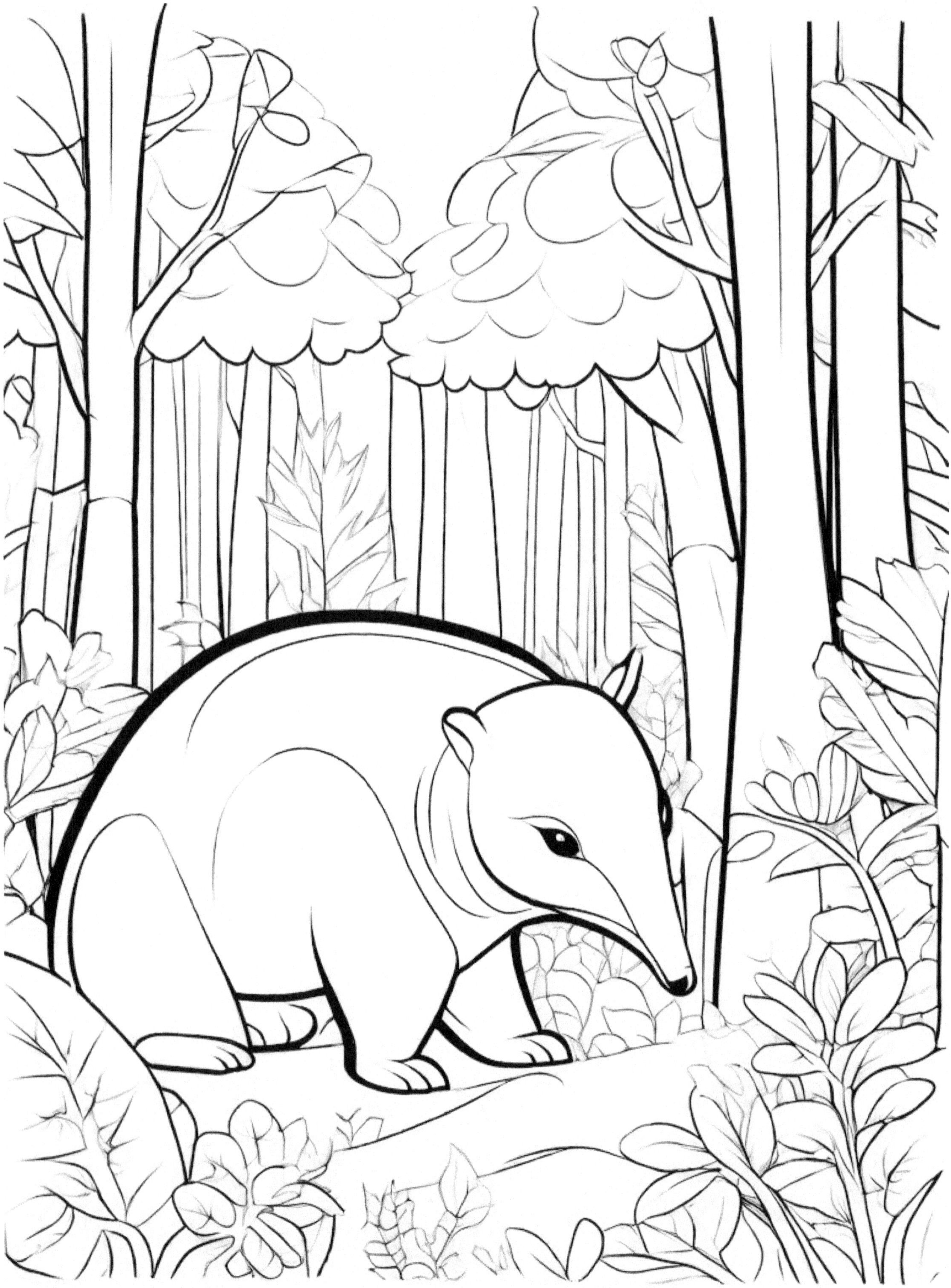

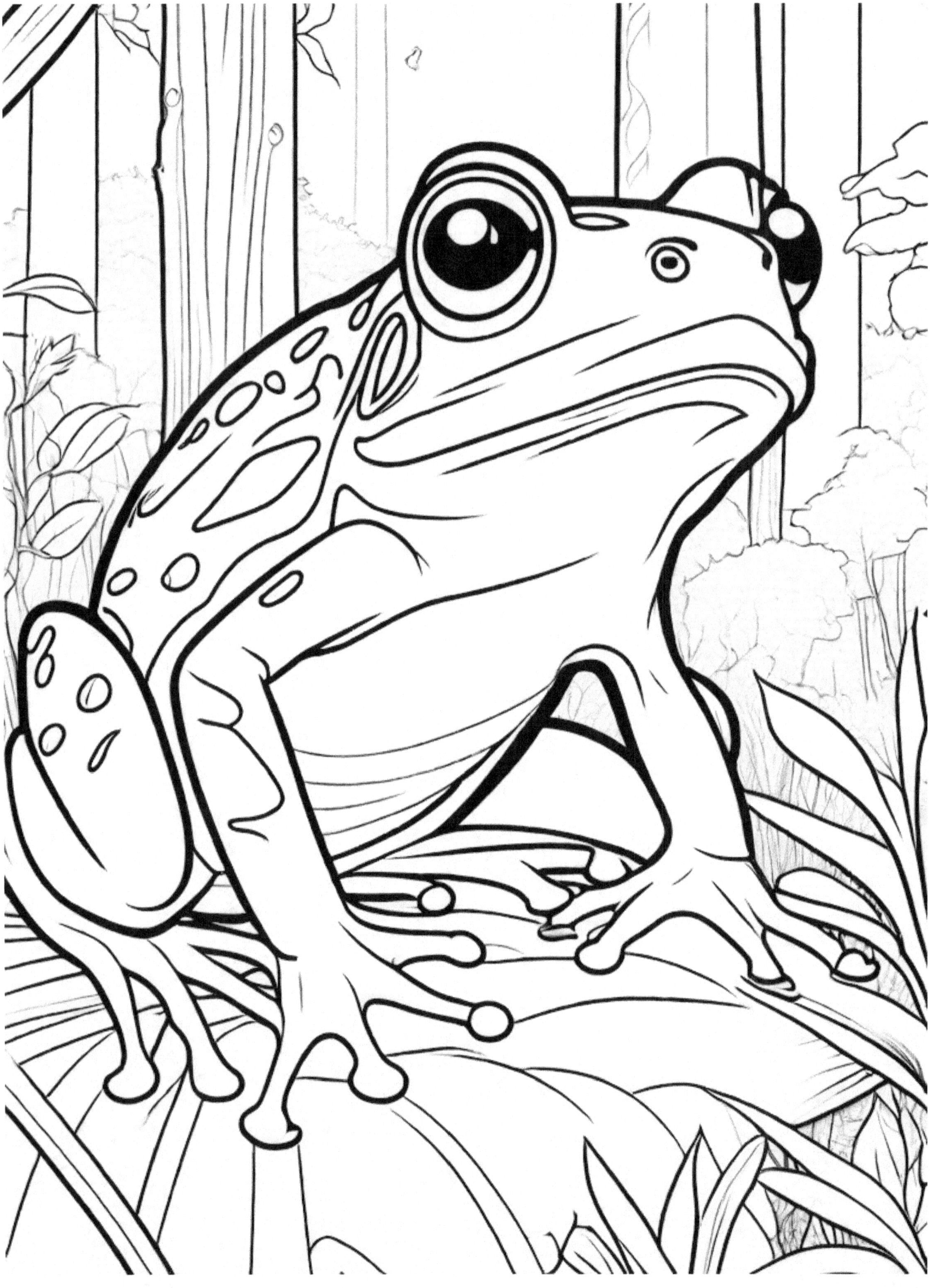

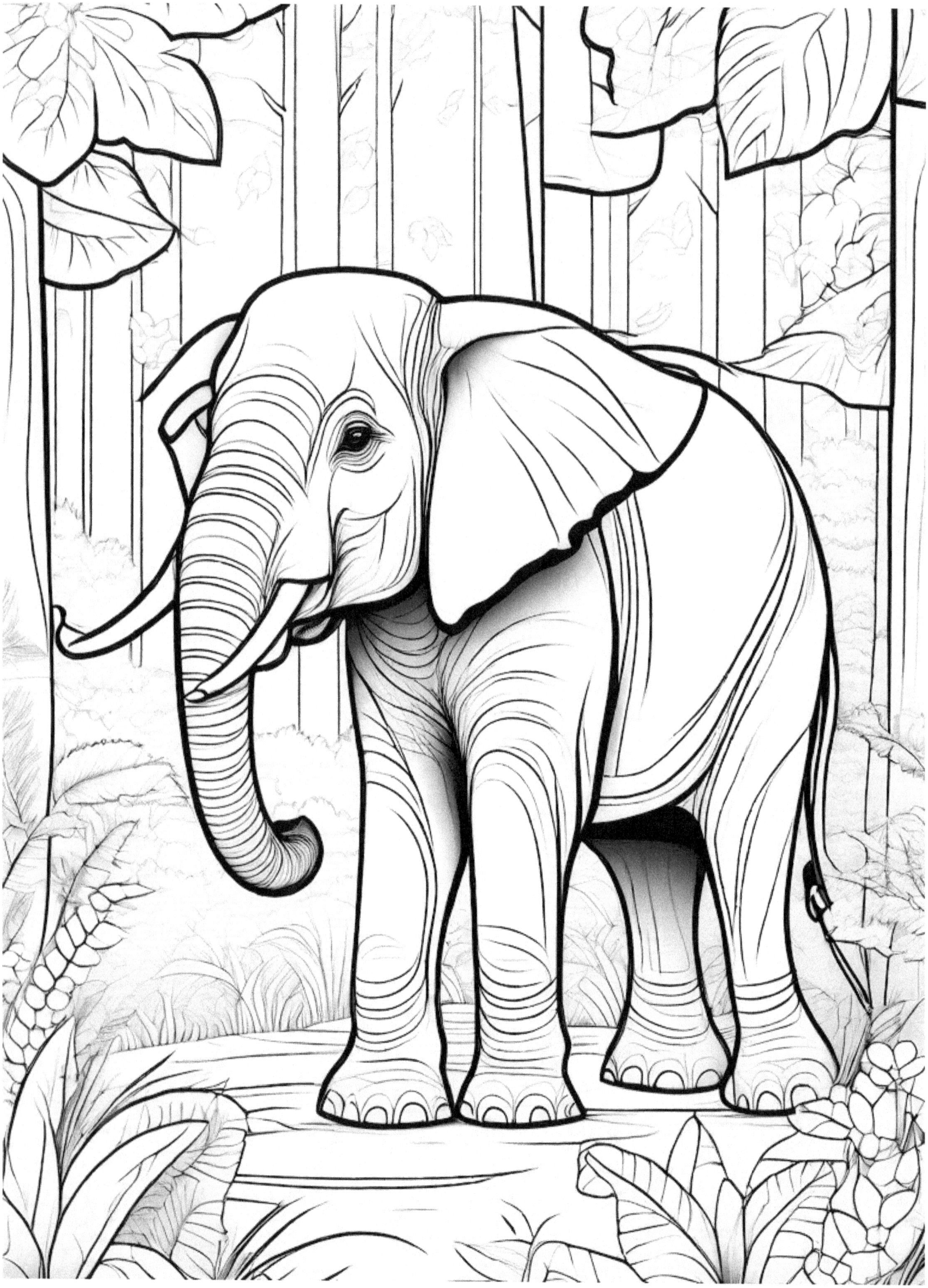

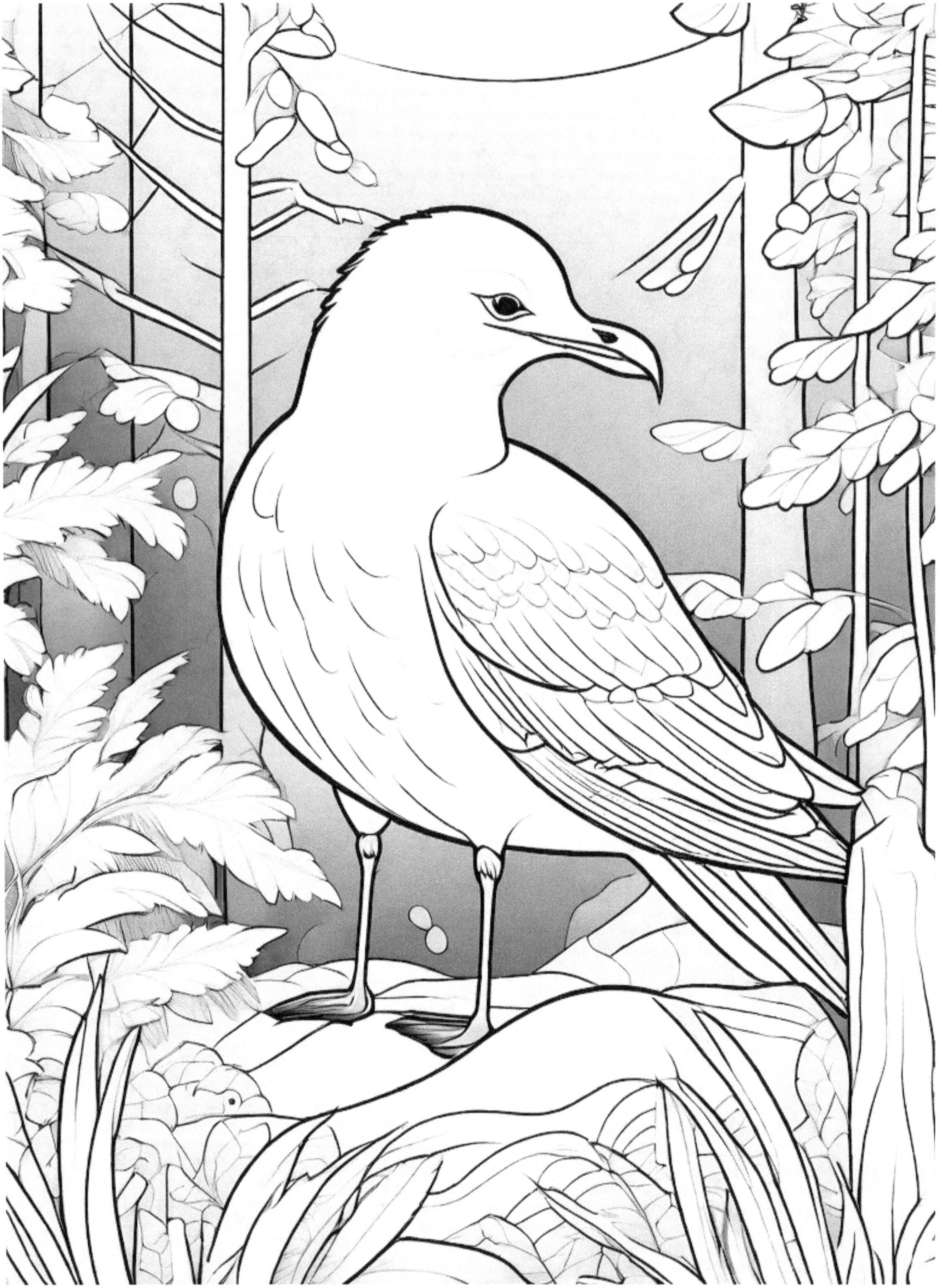

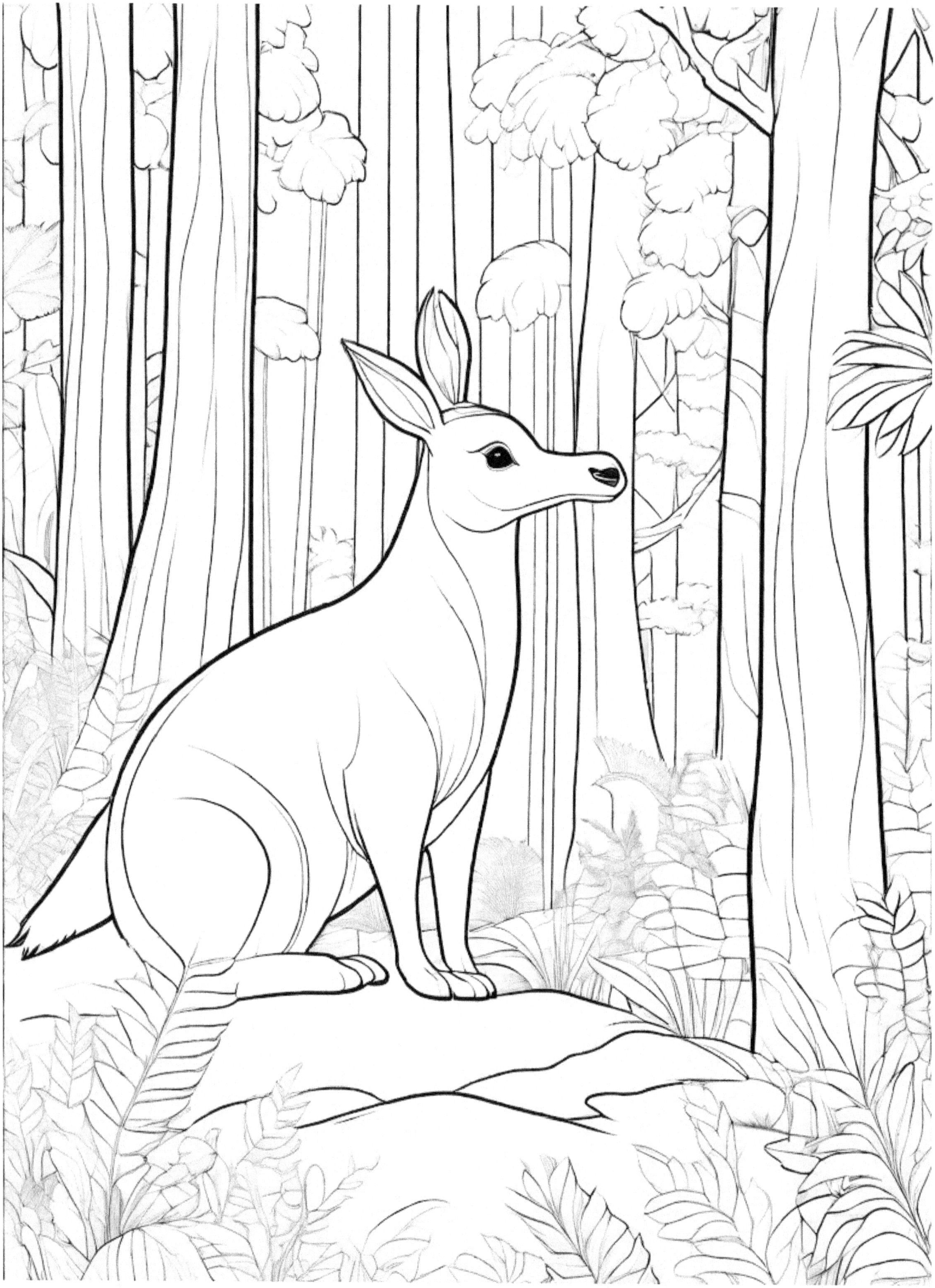

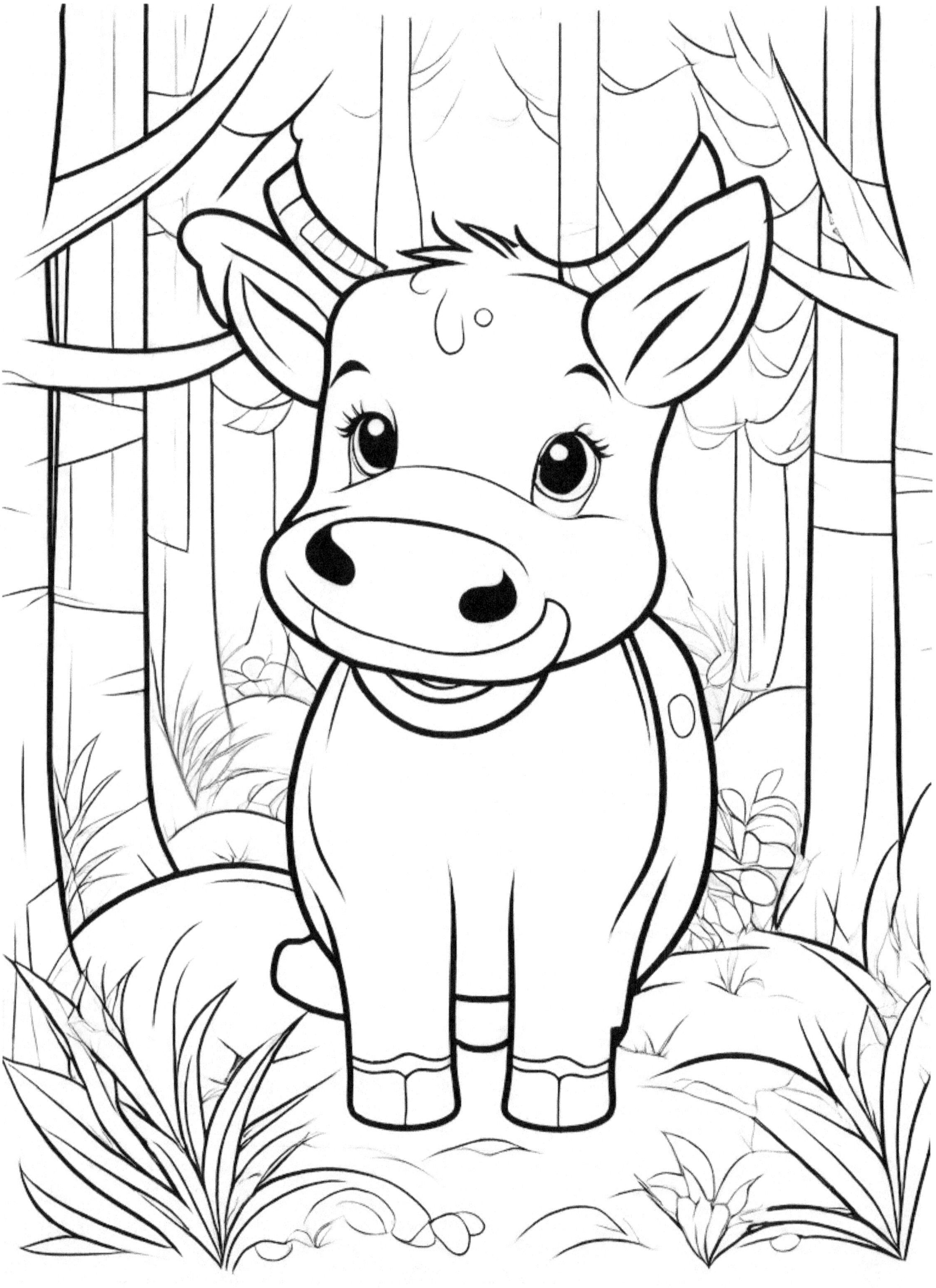

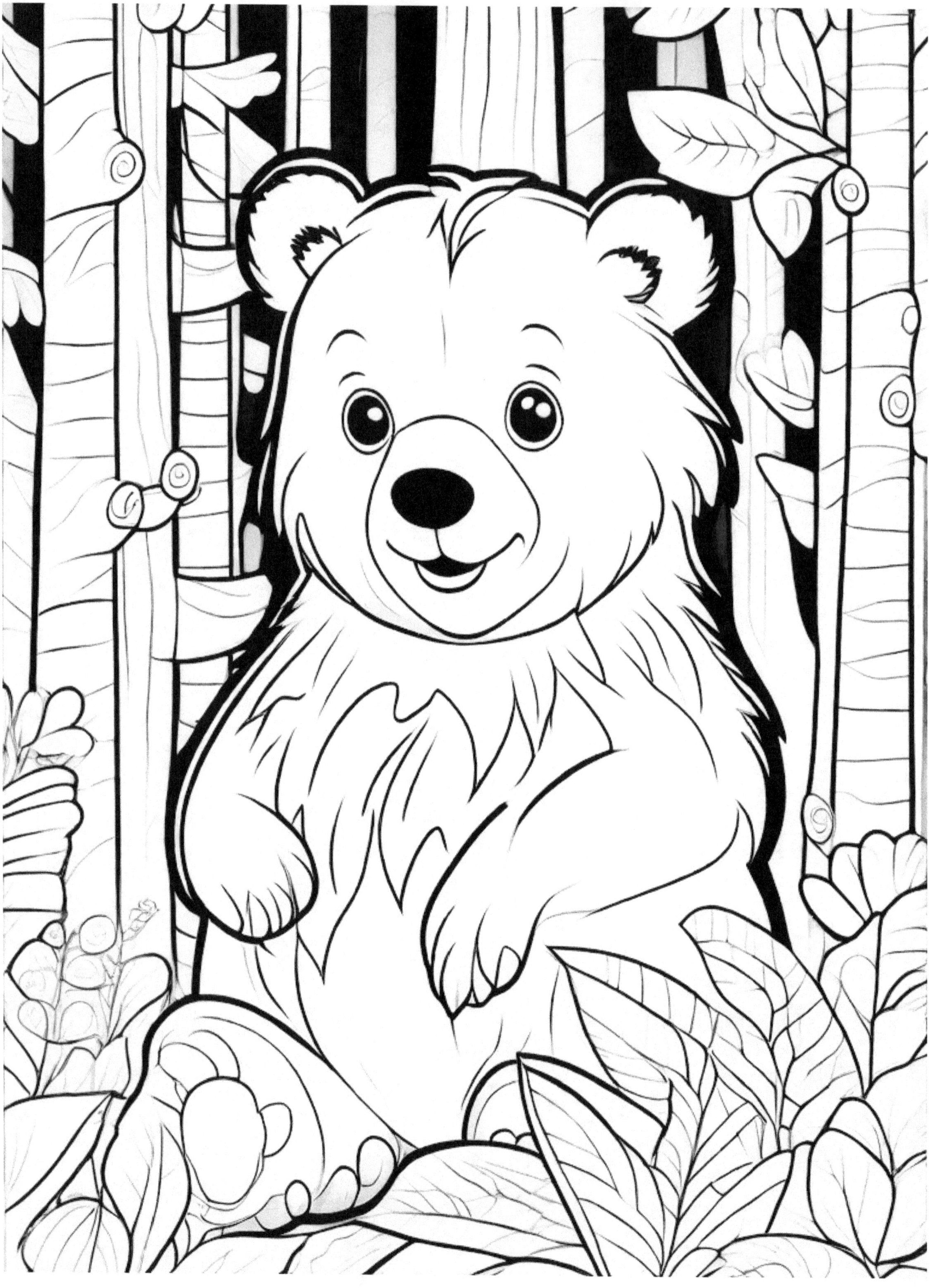

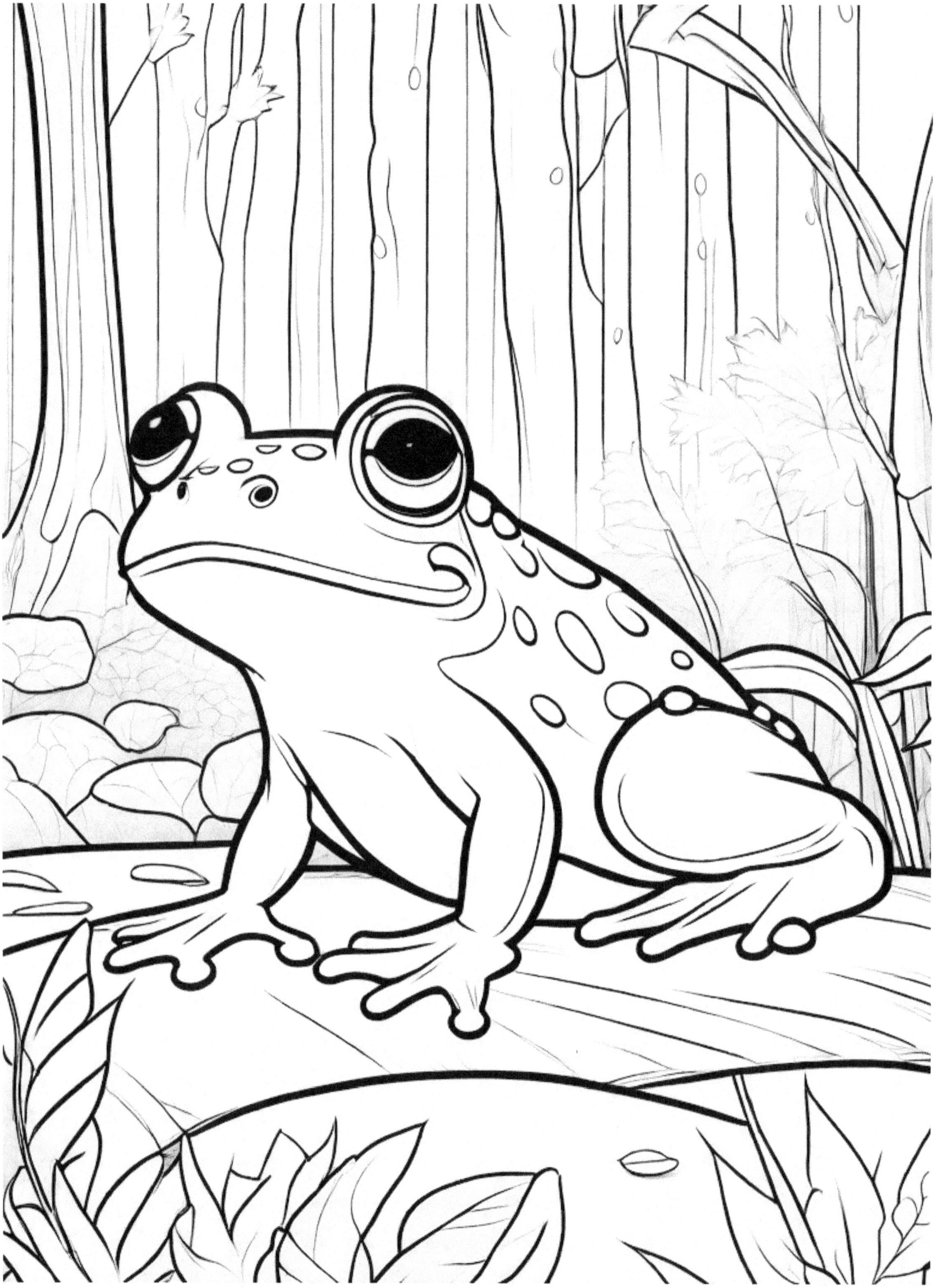

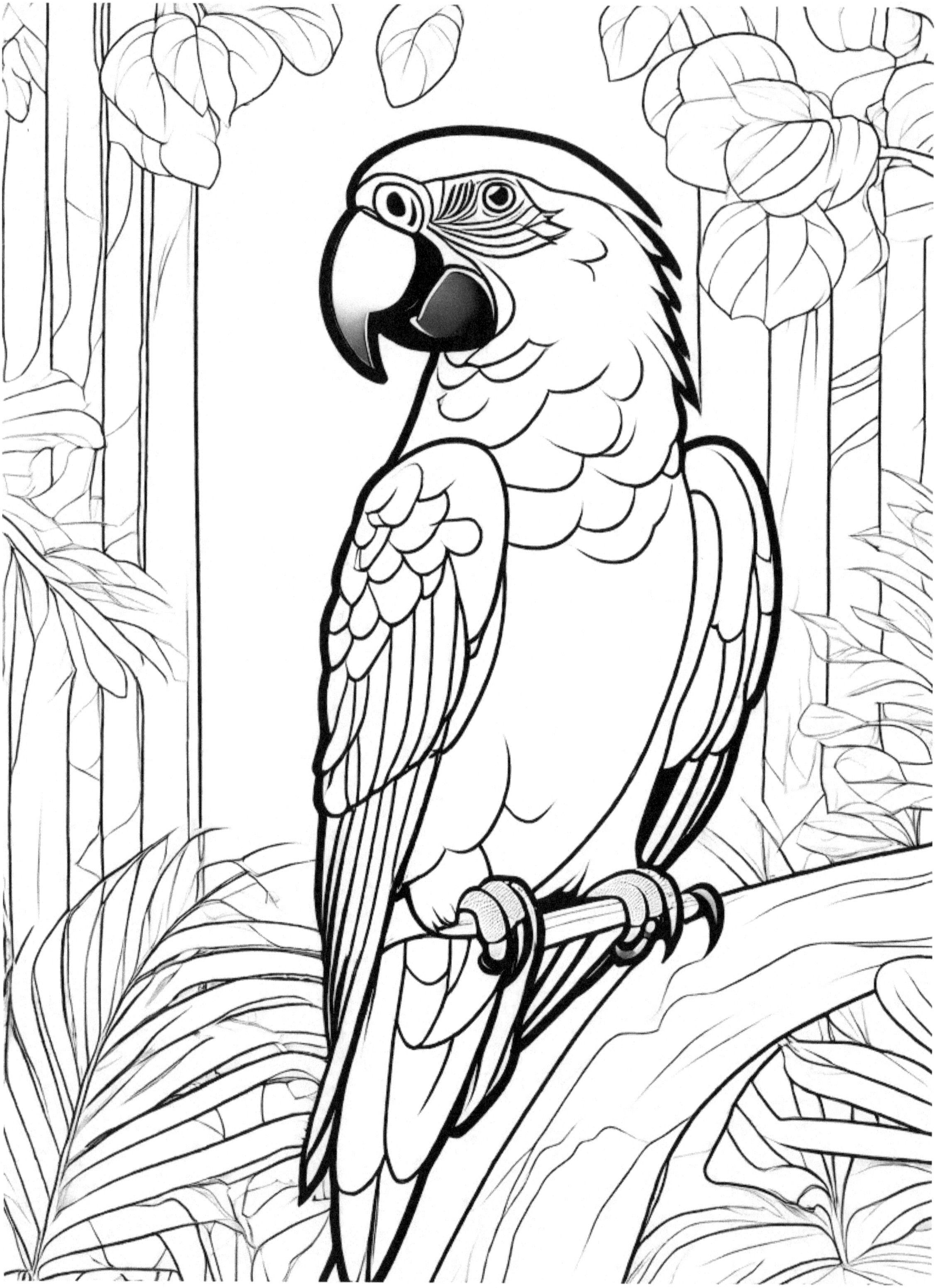

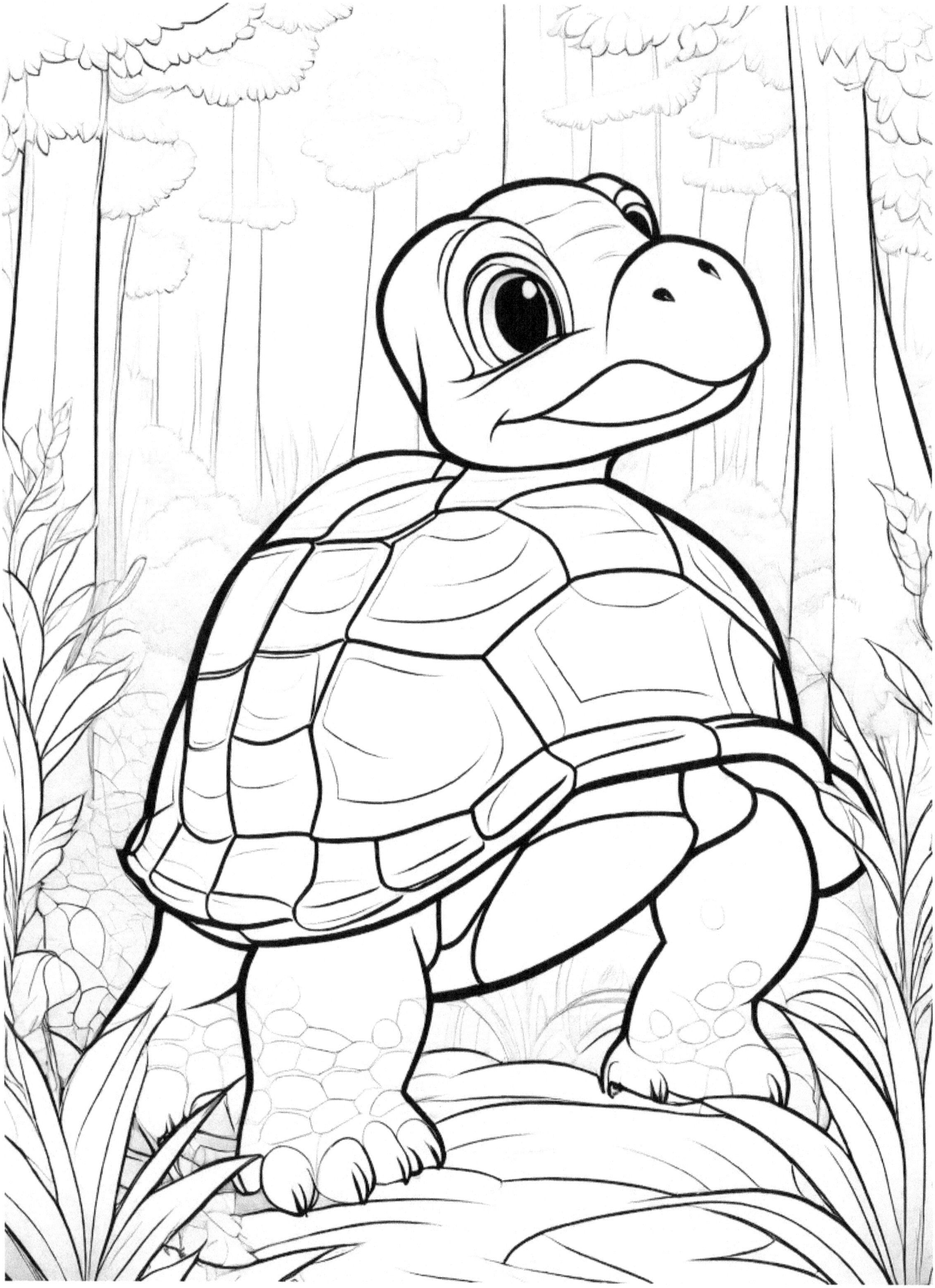

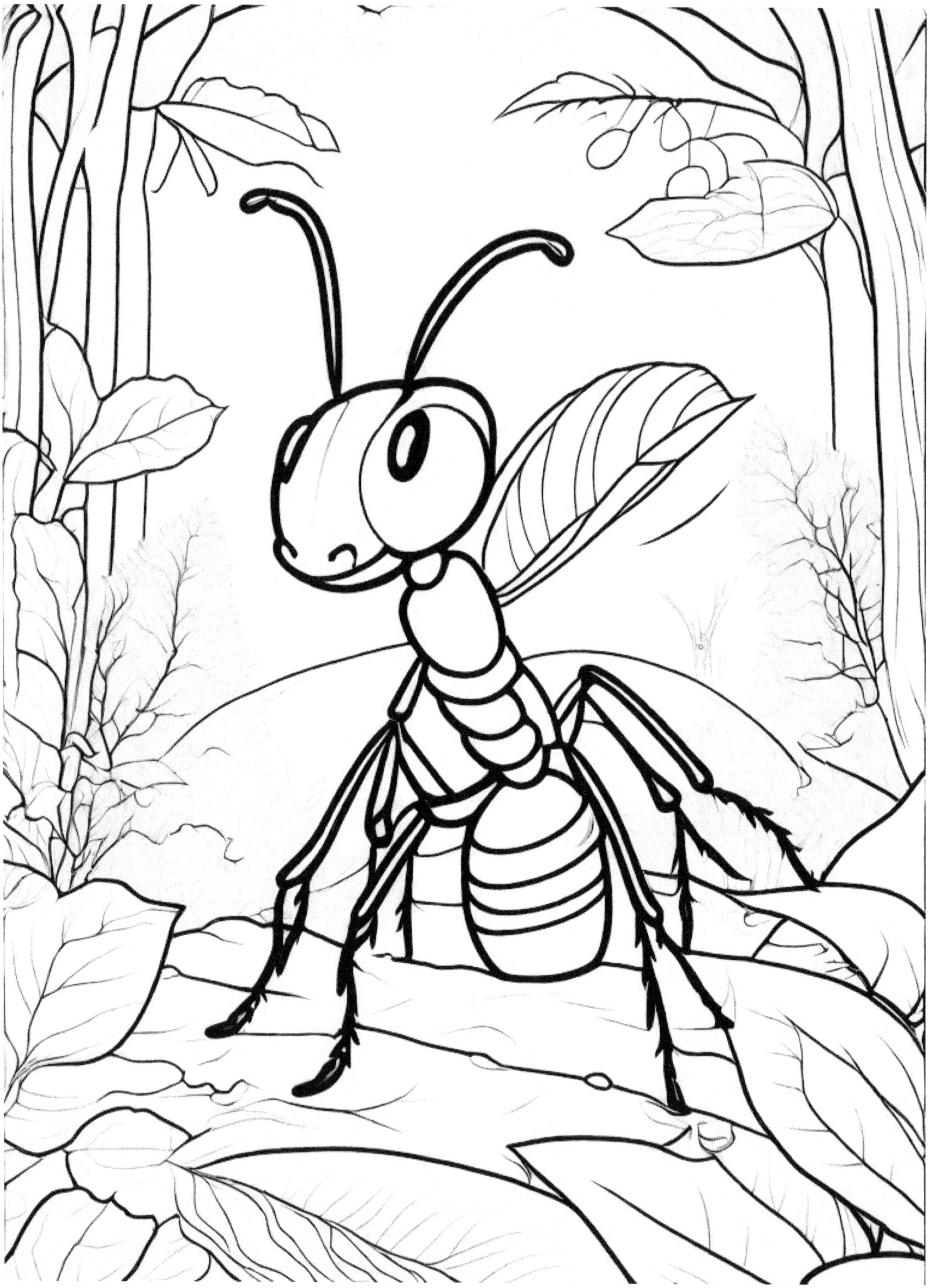

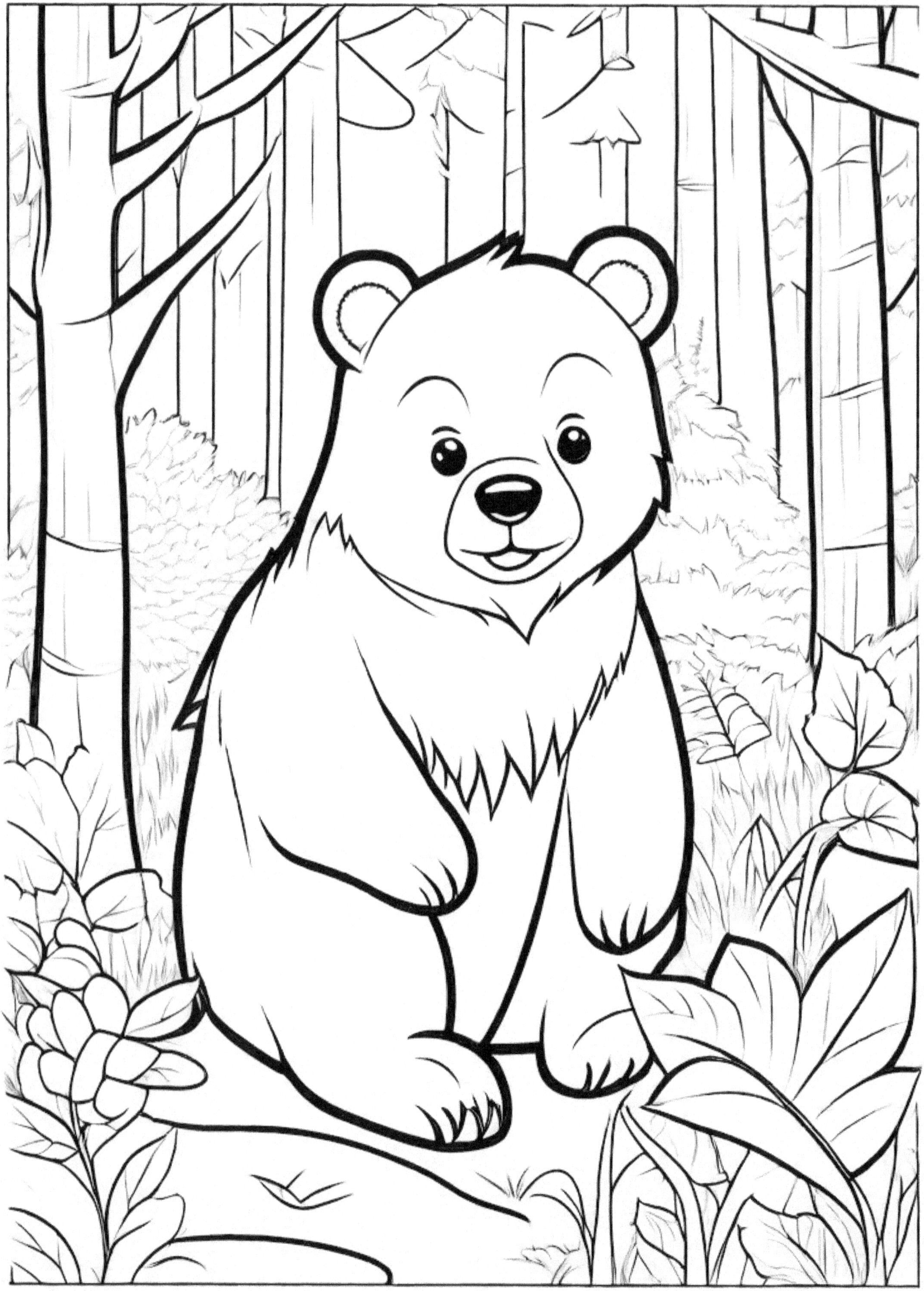

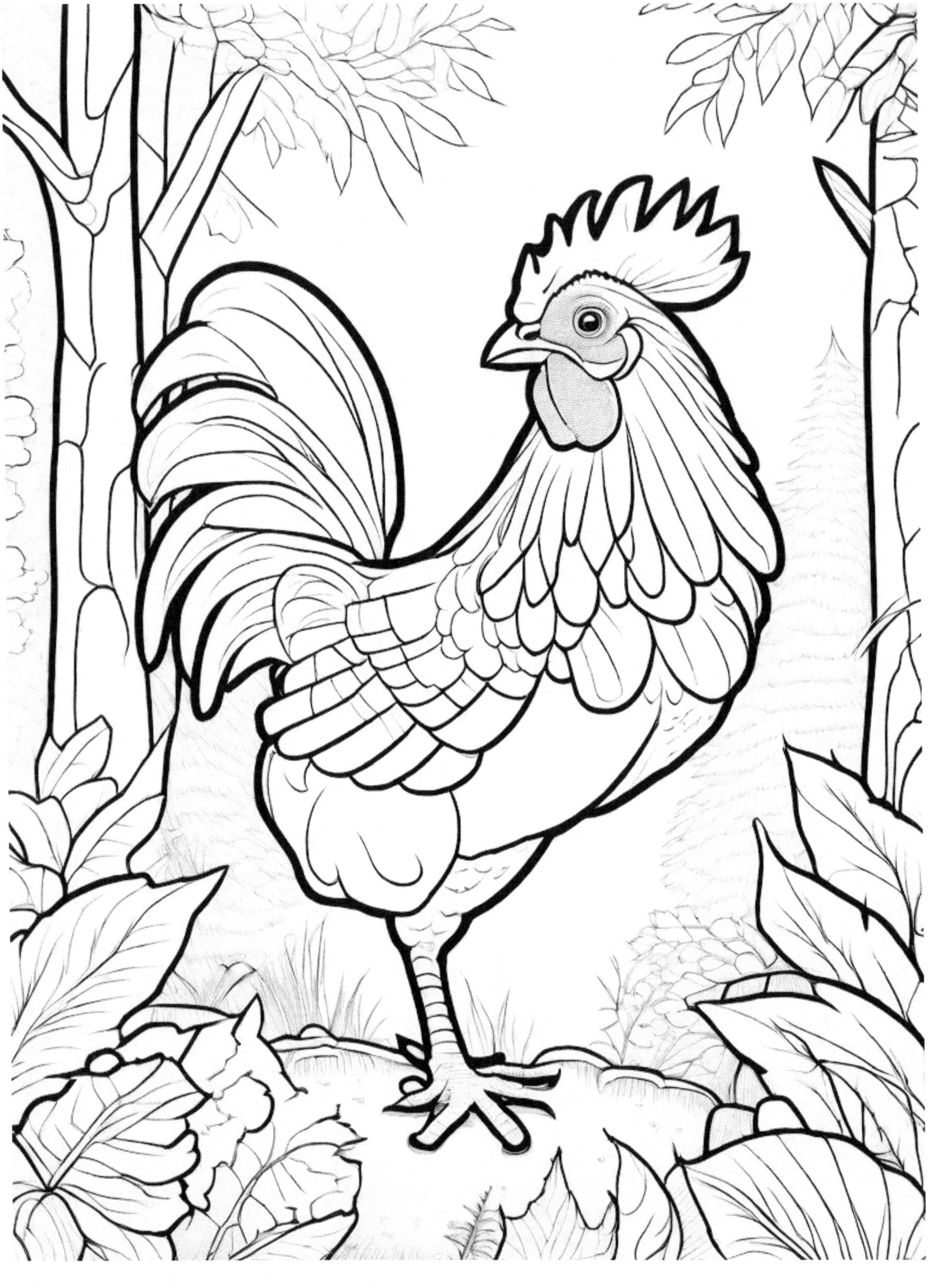

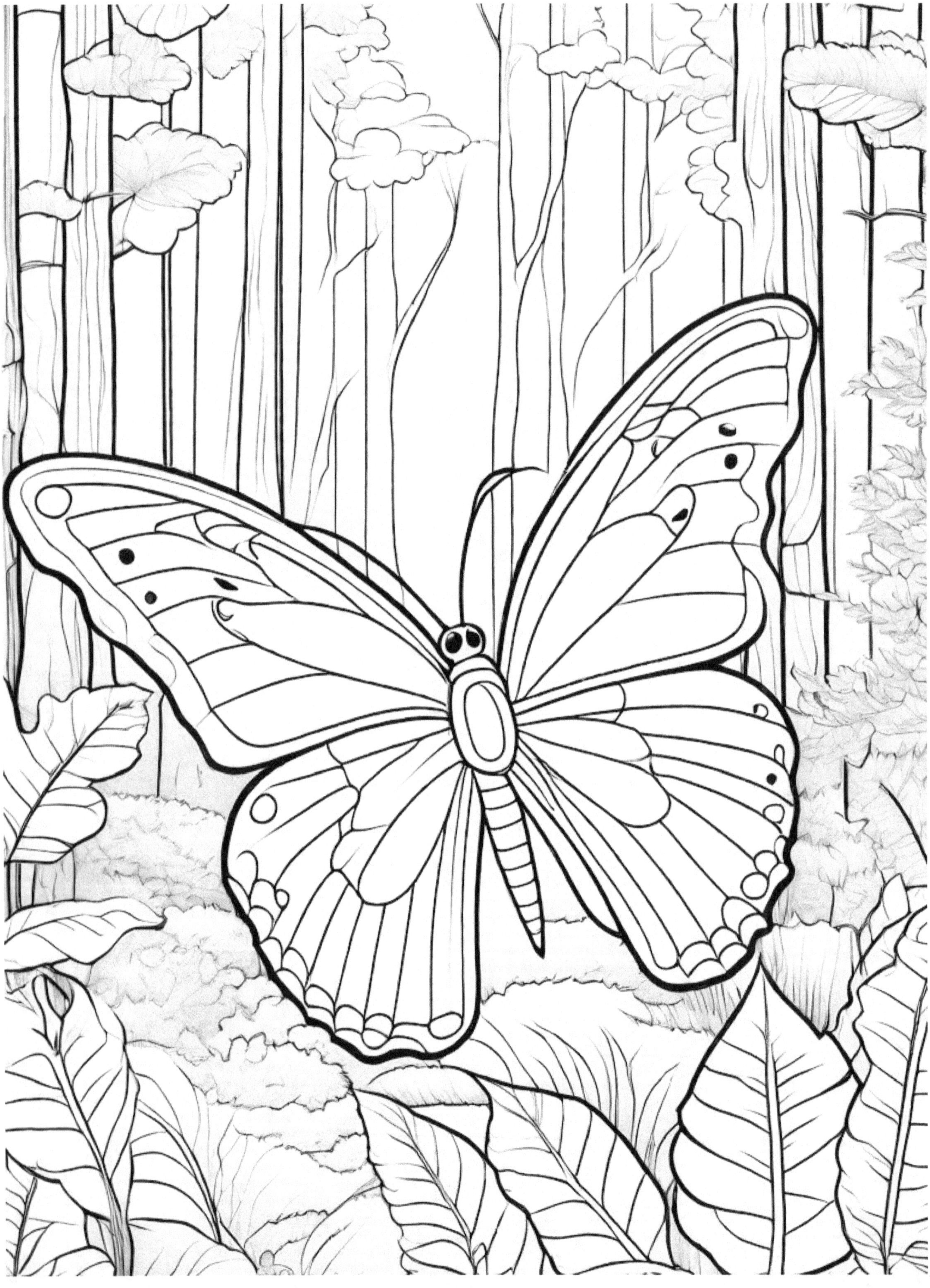

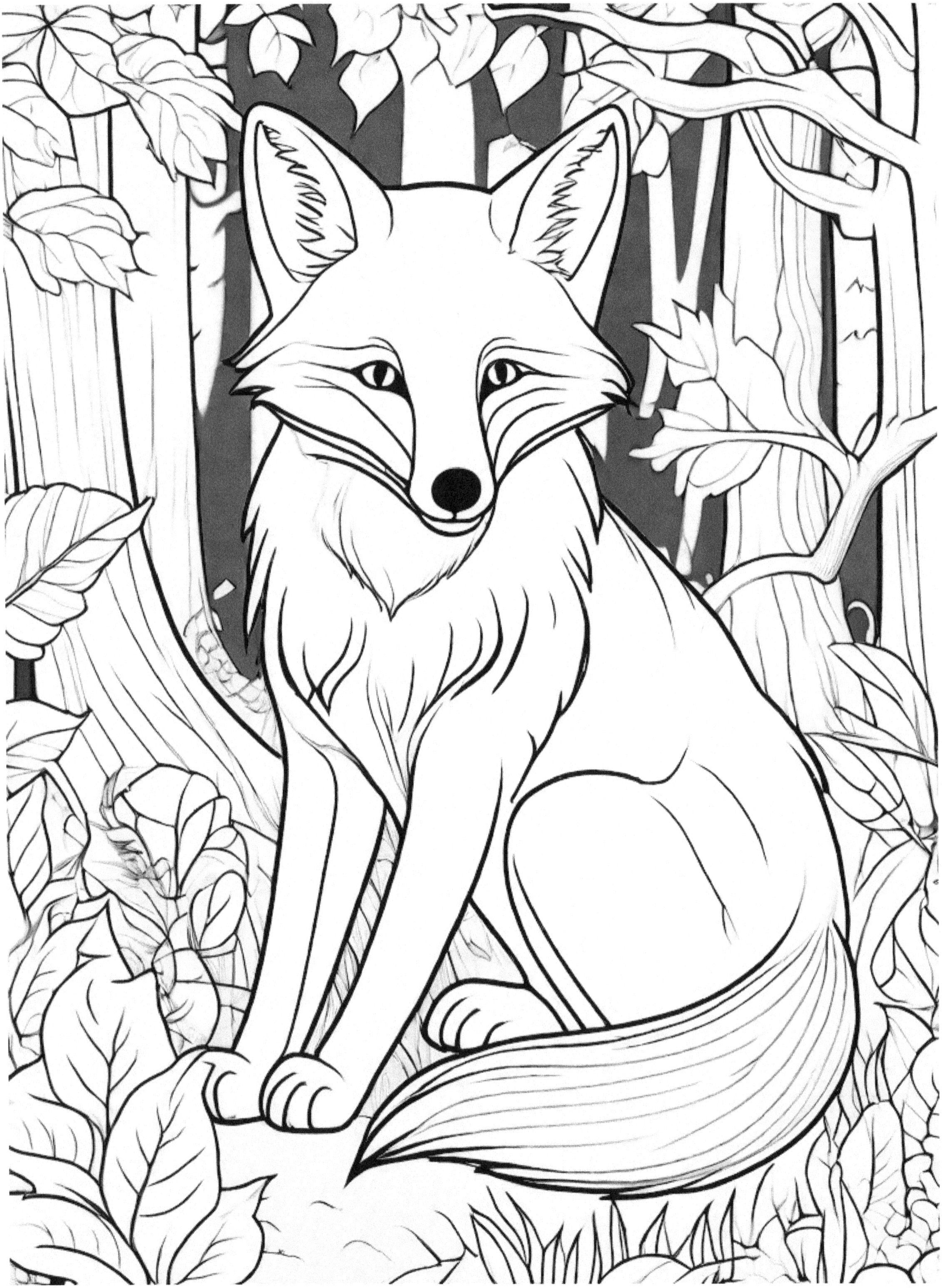

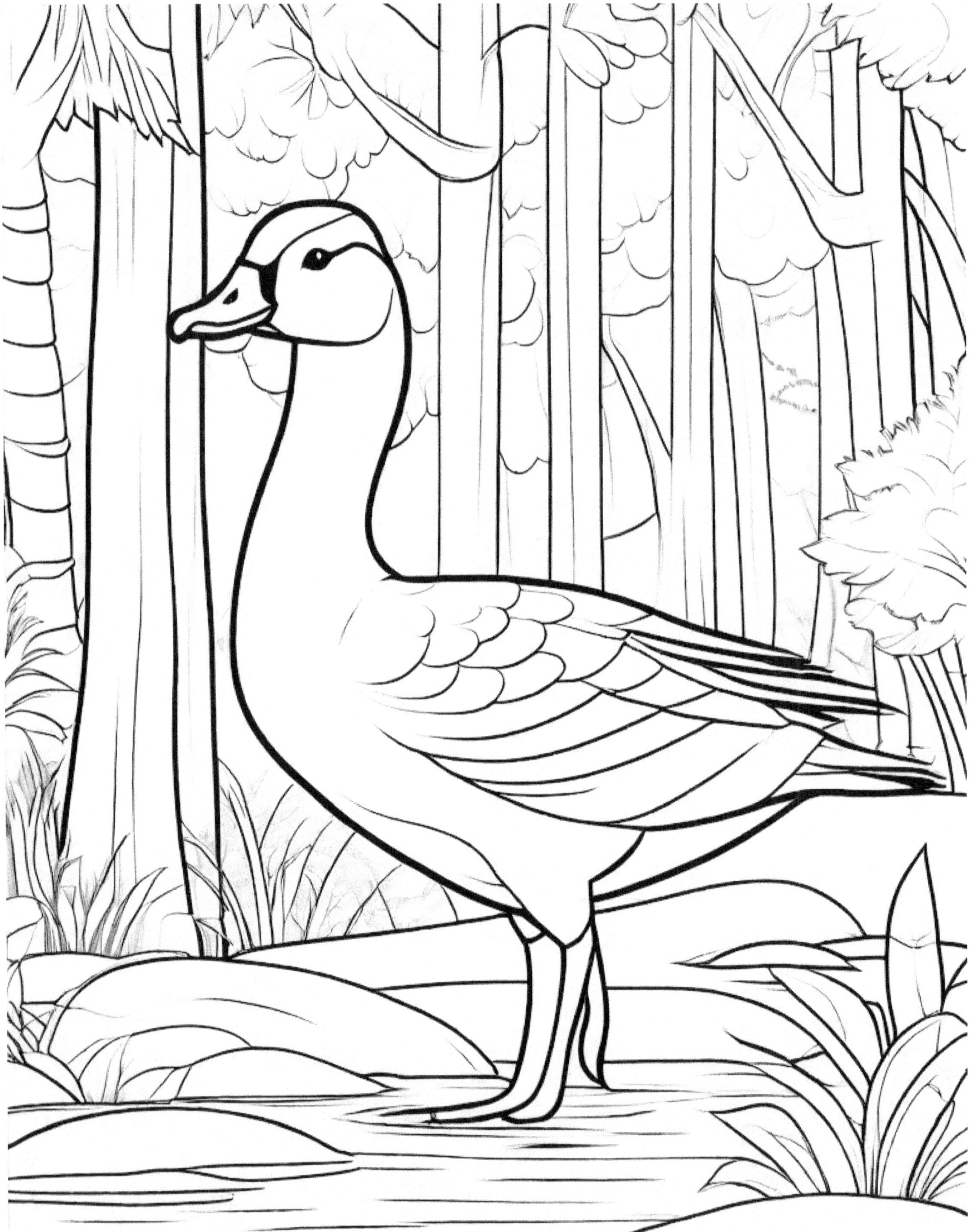

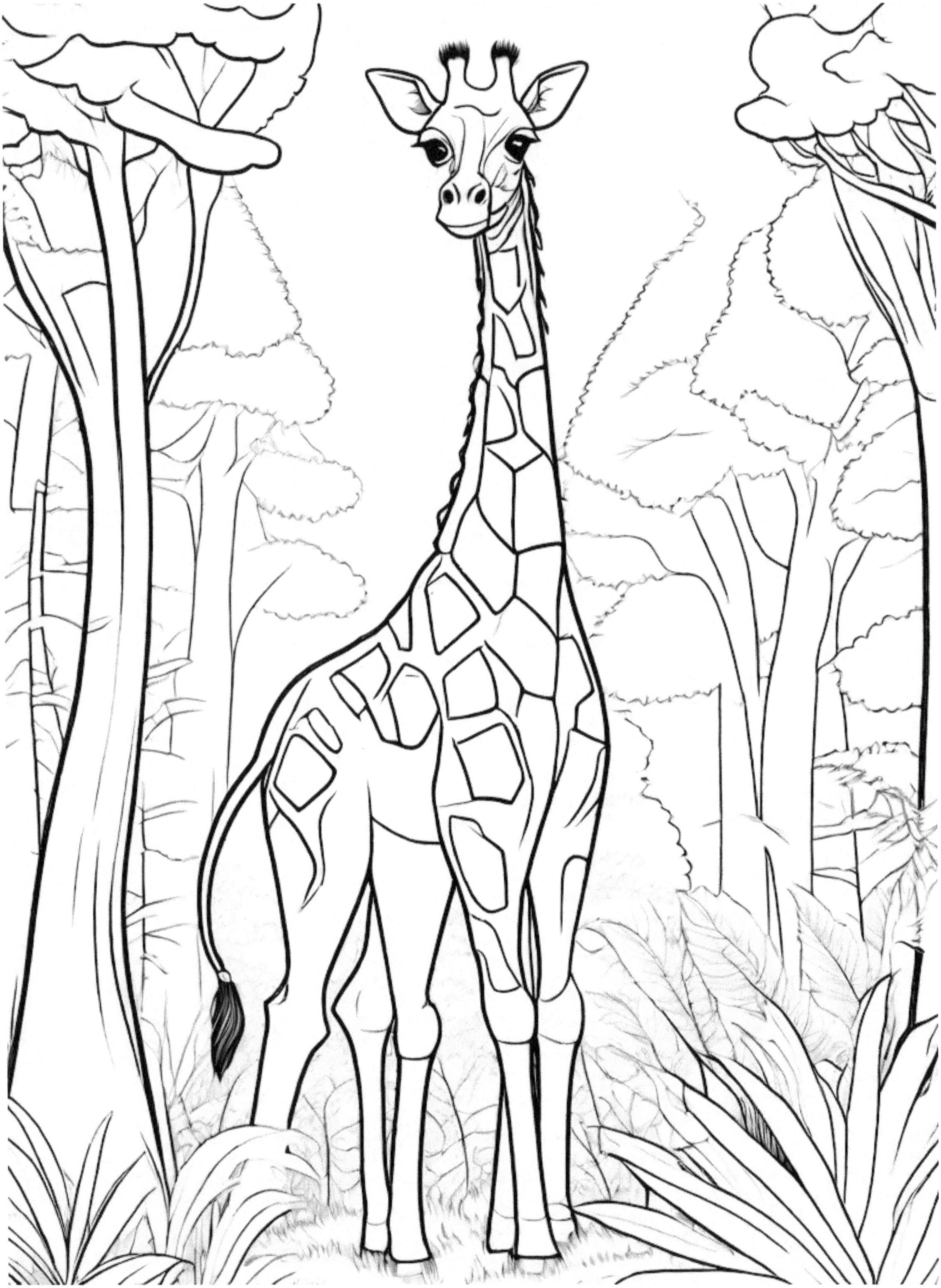

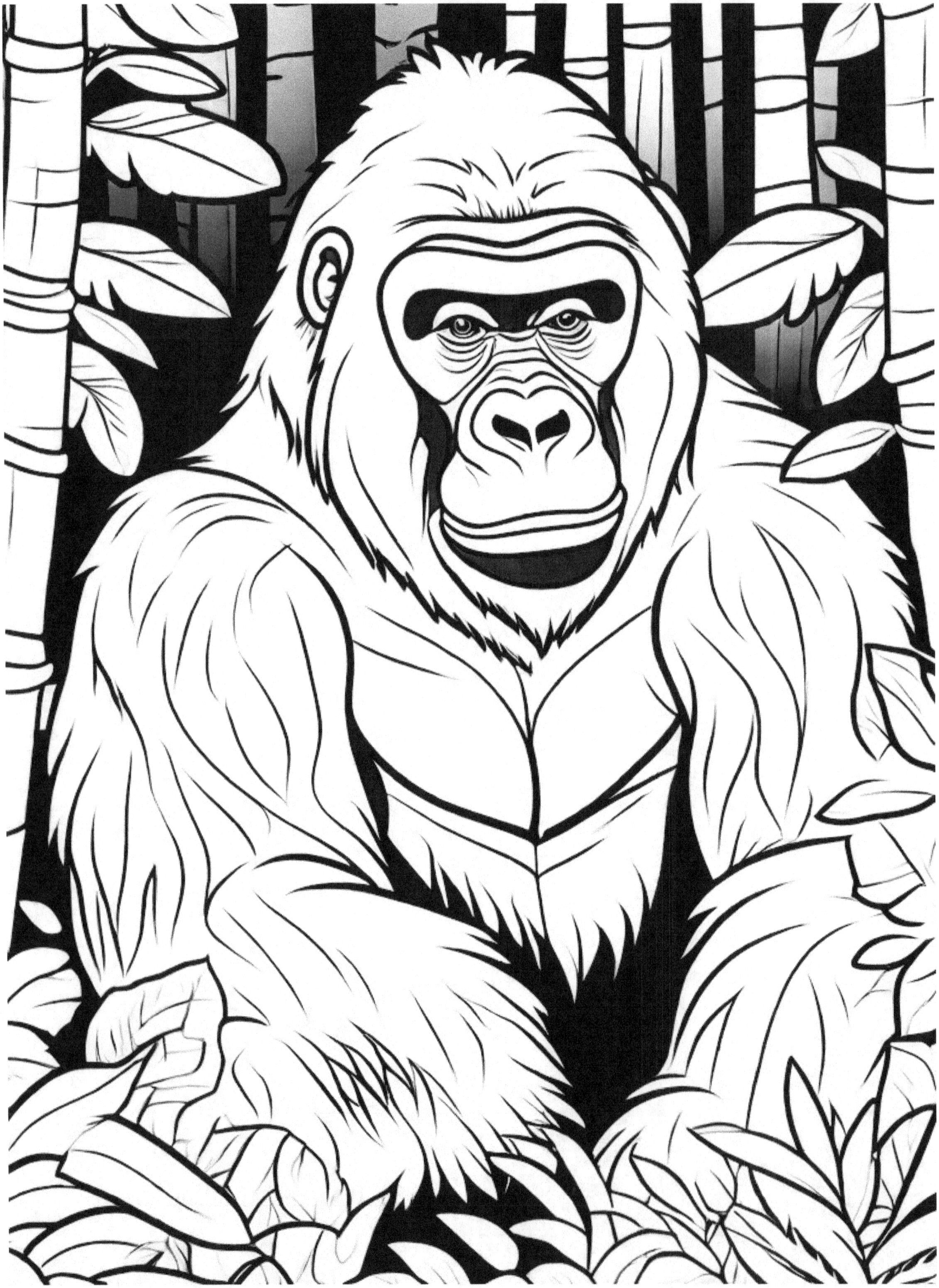

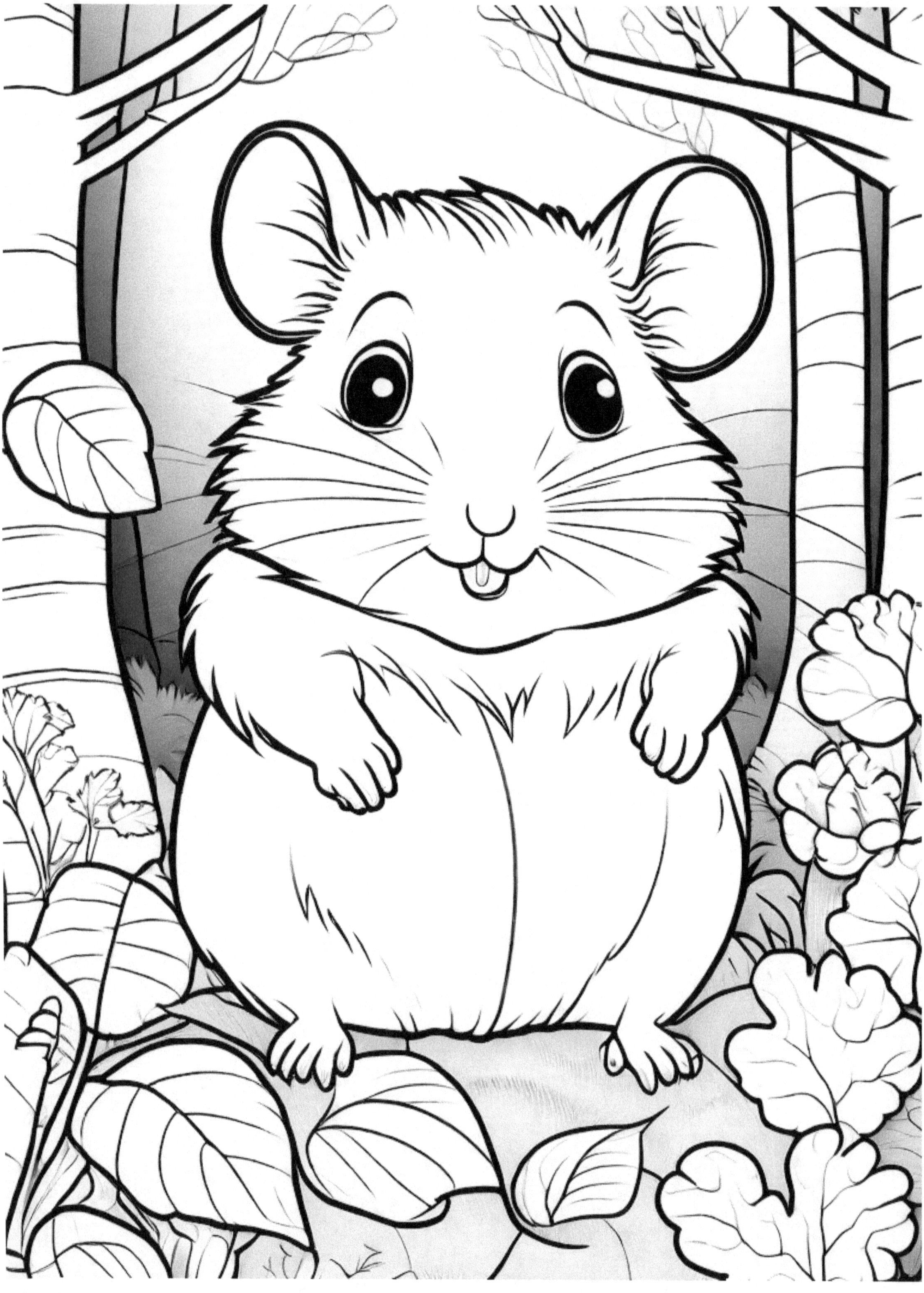

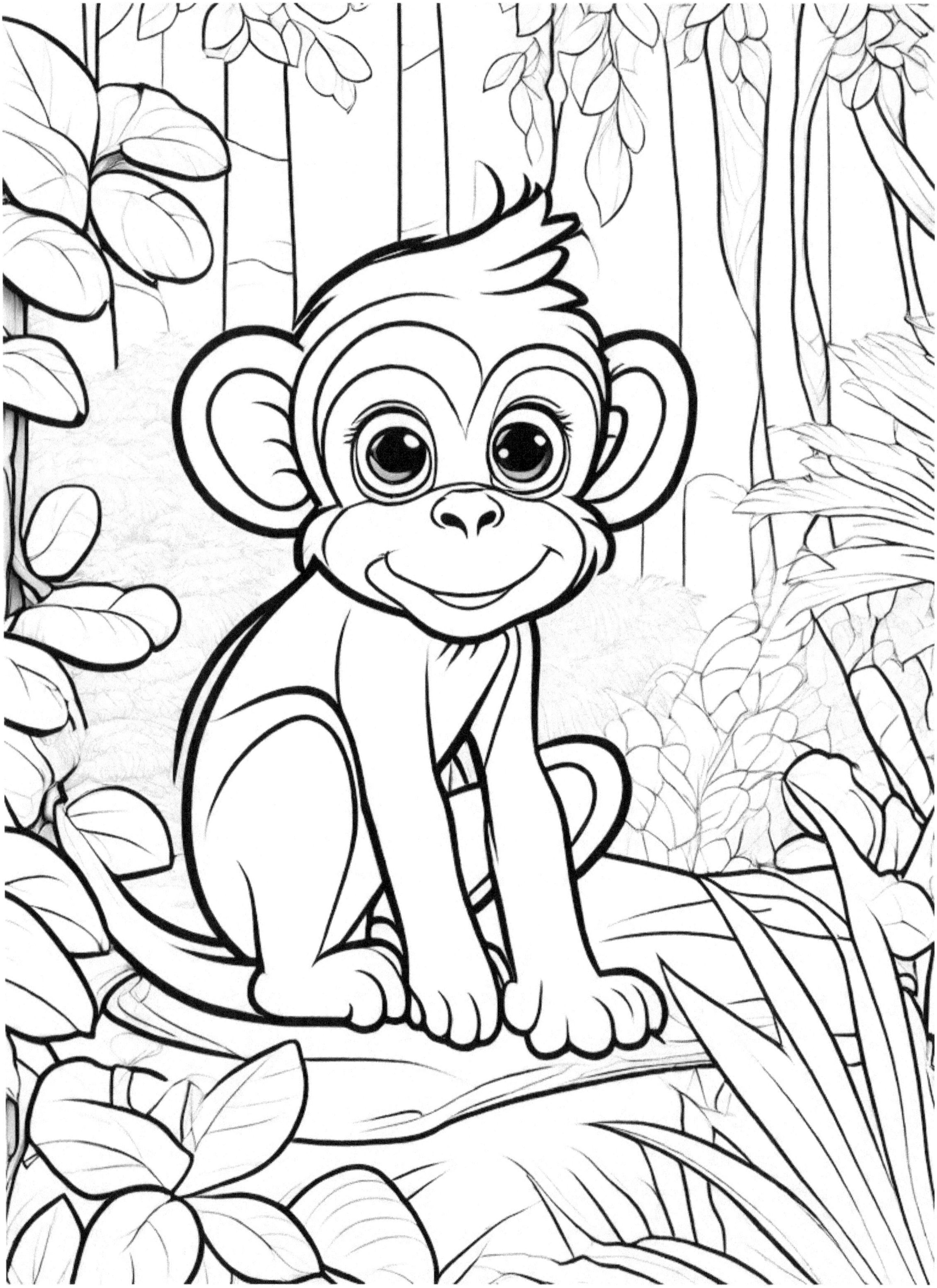

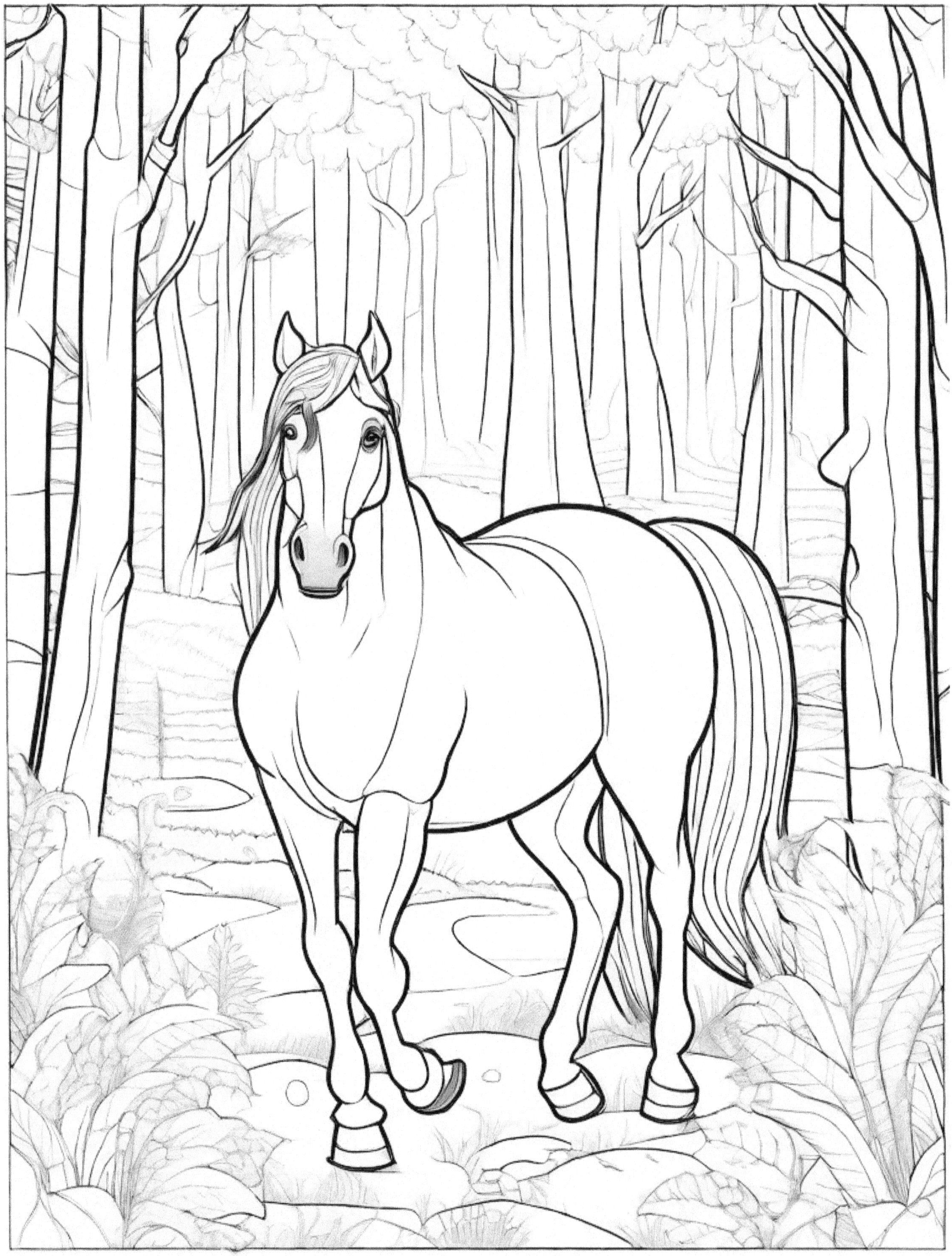

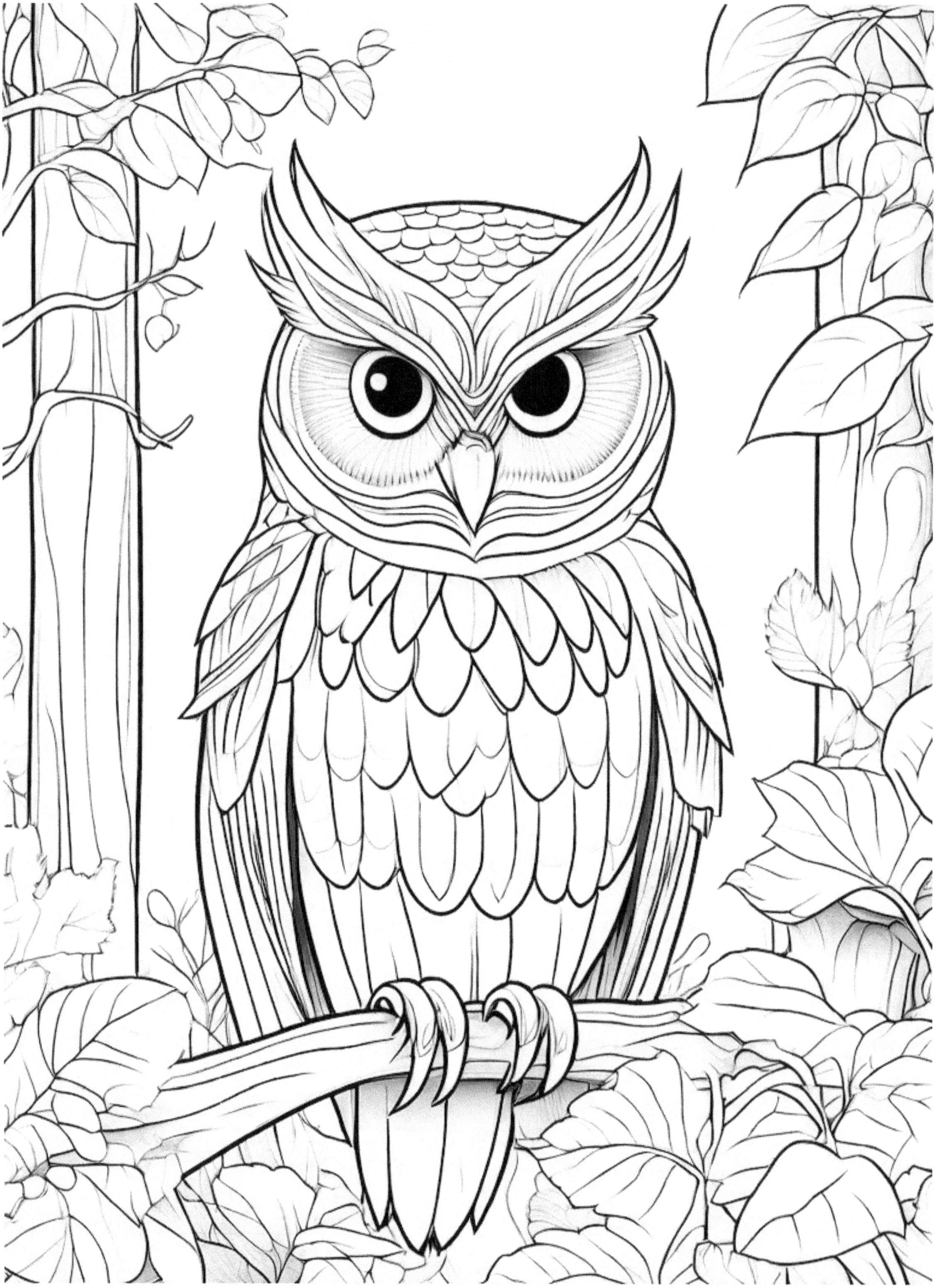

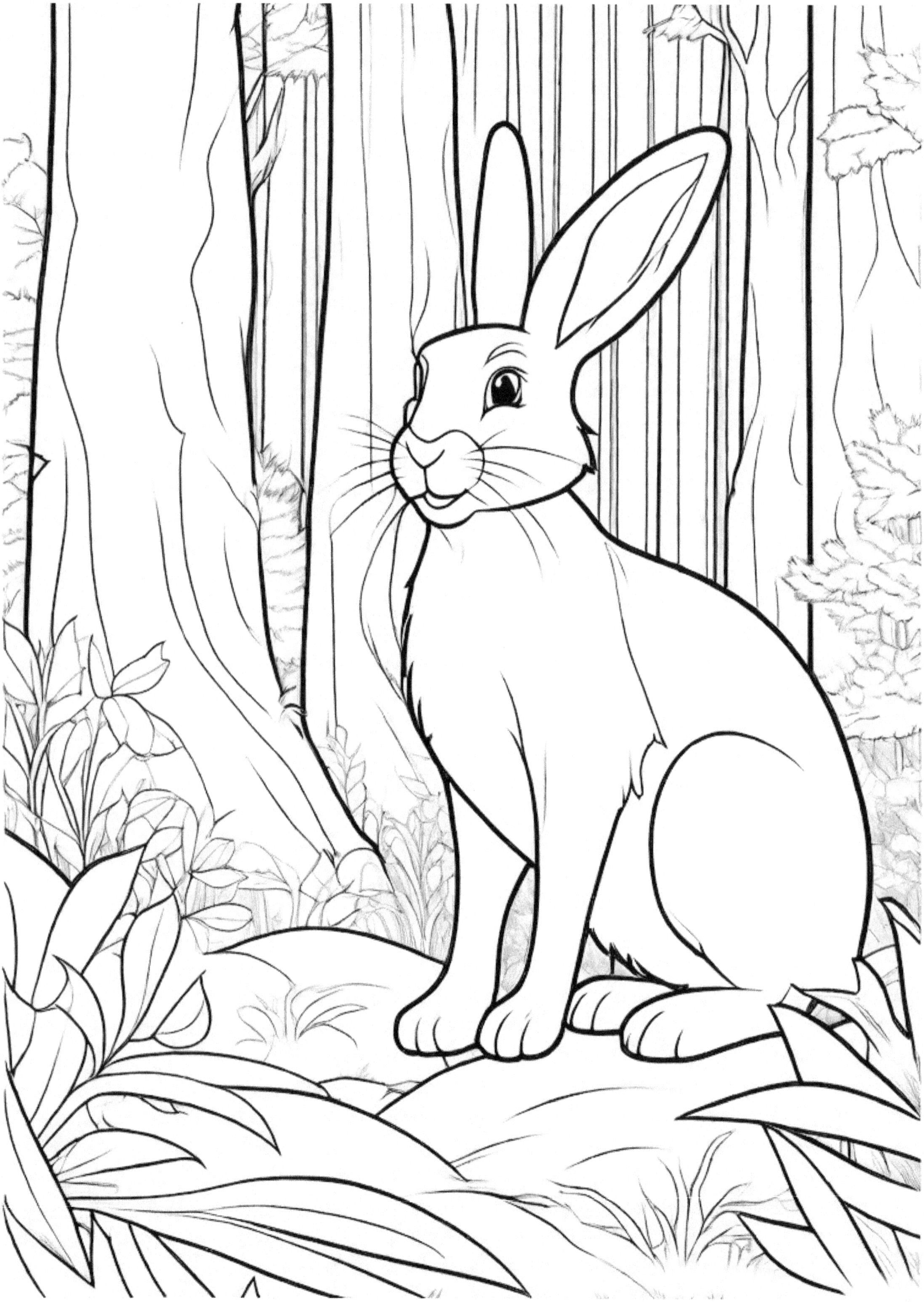

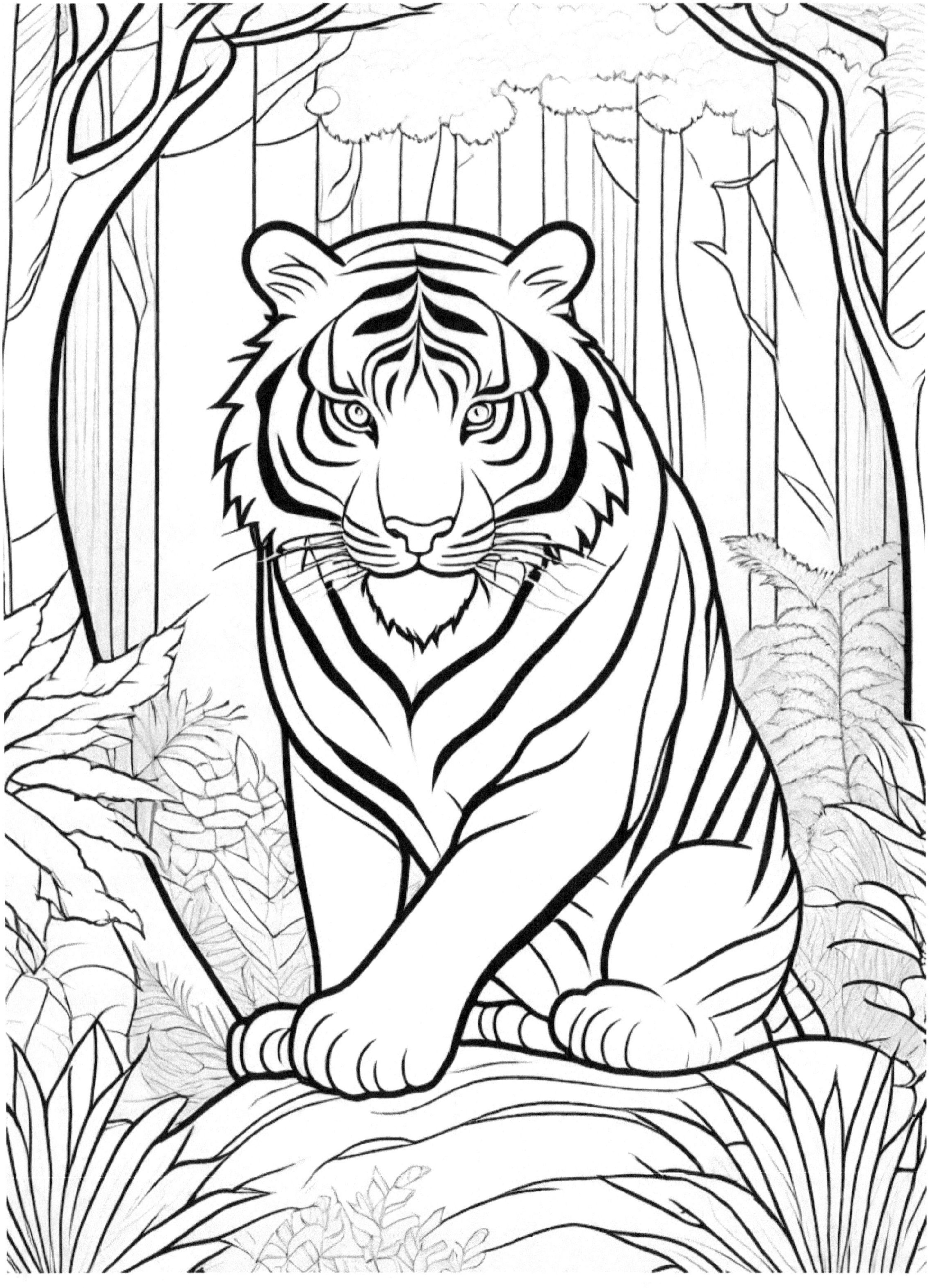

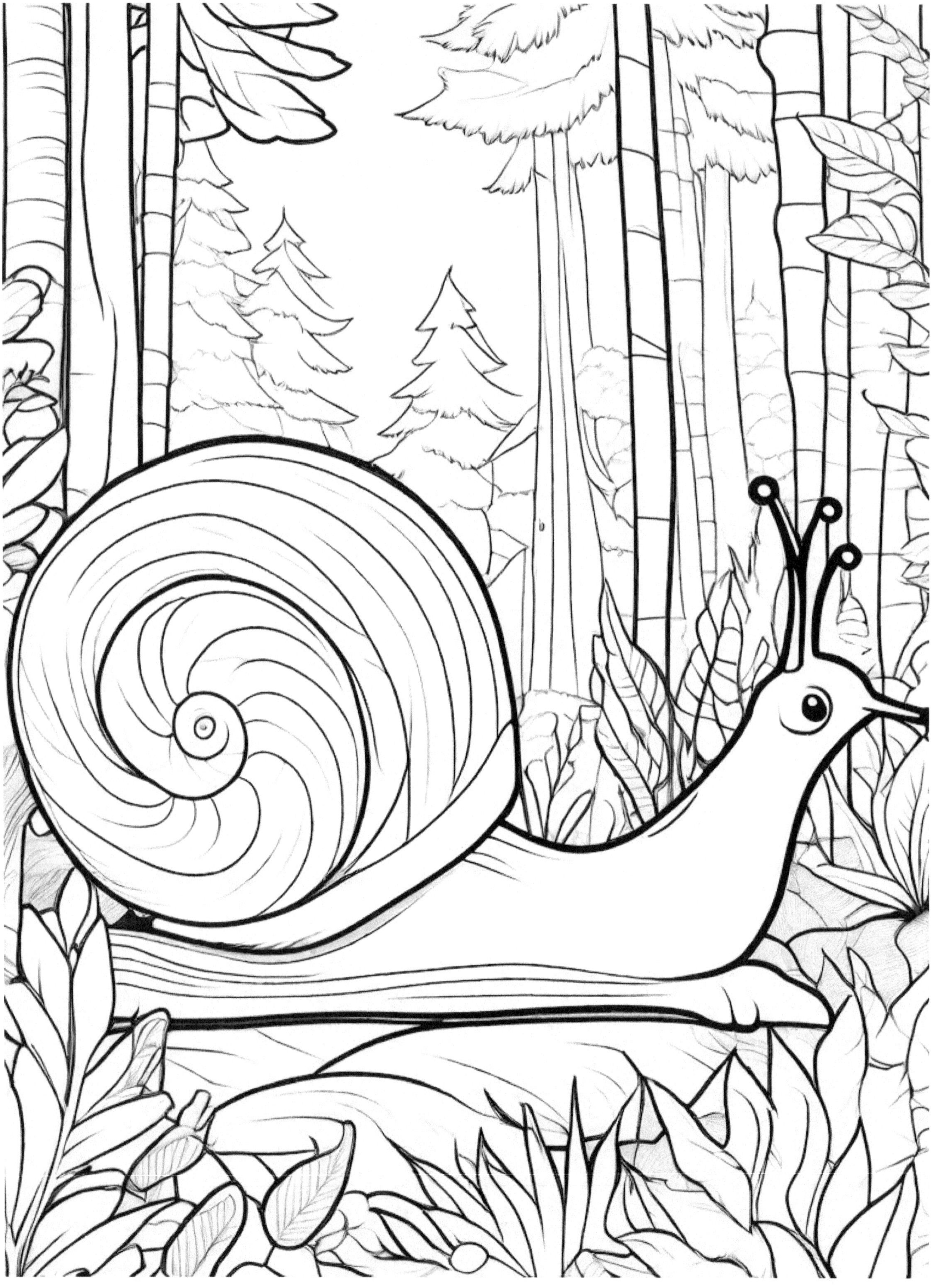

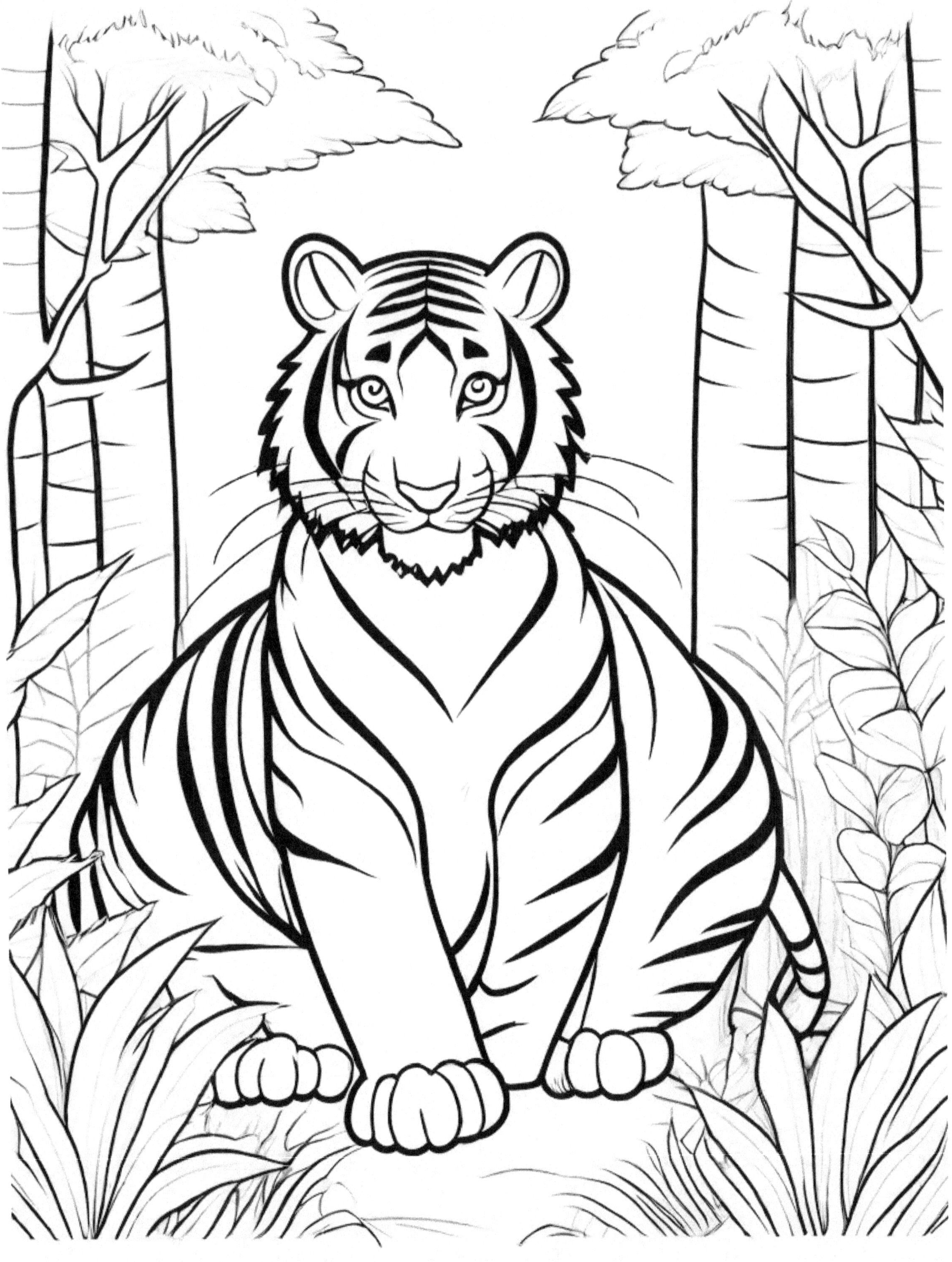

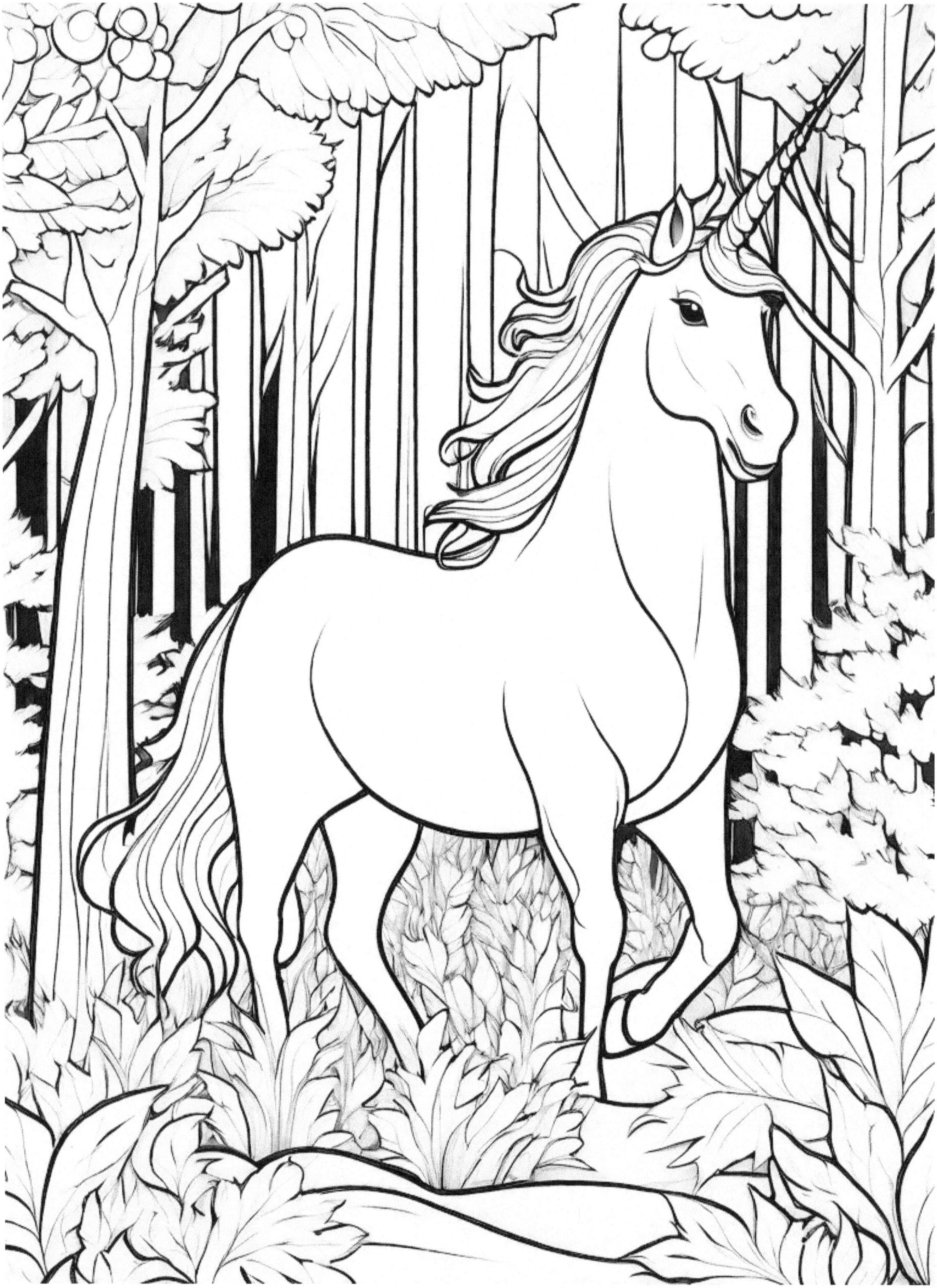

www.ingramcontent.com/pod-product-compliance
Lightning Source LLC
Chambersburg PA
CBHW080940260726
48661CB00010B/4015
* 9 7 9 8 8 7 1 3 2 3 9 5 3 *